New Revised 4th Edition
VACATION,
RETIREMENT & LEISURE
HOME PLANS

PUBLISHER JAMES D. MCNAIR III
COVER PHOTOGRAPHY BY BETH SINGER • COVER DESIGN BY PAULA MENNONE

LIBRARY OF CONGRESS NO.: 94-073701
ISBN: 0-938708-61-9

GARLINGHOUSE

© 1995 by The L.F. Garlinghouse Co., Inc of Middletown, Connecticut. Building a house from a design in this publication without first purchasing a set of home plans is a copyright violation. Printed in the USA.

Submit all *Canadian* plan orders to:
The Garlinghouse Company
20 Cedar Street North
Kitchener, Ontario N2H 2WB

Canadian Orders Only: 1-800-561-4169
Fax #: 1-519-743-1282
Customer Service #: 1-519-743-4169

PHOTOGRAPHY BY JOHN EHRENCLOU

Cozy Homestead

DESIGN 24651

★ Main floor	1,821 sq. ft.
★ Basement	1,075 sq. ft.
★ Garage	742 sq. ft.
★ Bedrooms	Three
★ Baths	2(Full)
★ Foundation	Basement

REFER TO PRICE CODE C

An
EXCLUSIVE DESIGN
By Plan One Homes, Inc.

*M*ulti-paned windows and a country porch set the theme for this comfortable home. The spacious living room is enhanced by the natural light from the front window and the fireplace with built-in bookshelves flanking one side. Formal entertaining will be a pleasure because the living room and formal dining room flow into each other and the kitchen is located next to the dining room. The efficient U-shaped kitchen includes a walk-in pantry and a double sink. A breakfast nook is provided with a convenient first floor laundry room to the left. The bedrooms have been designed to insure the privacy of the master suite. The master suite includes such luxurious amenities as a whirlpool tub, compartmented toilet, separate step-in shower, walk-in closet and a decorative tray ceiling. The two additional bedrooms are located at the opposite side of the home and share a full hall bath brightened by a skylight.

THIS PLAN HAS BEEN MODIFIED TO SUIT INDIVIDUAL TASTES.

Total Living Area:
1,821 sq. ft.

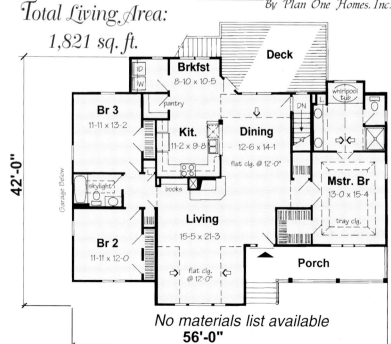

No materials list available
56'-0"

Rustic Charm & Good Looks

This hillside home, characterized by enormous rooms and two garages, is built on two levels. From the foyer, travel down one hall to a cozy bedroom, full bath, island kitchen, laundry and garage. Or, walk straight into the sun-filled Great room and dining room with a lovely wraparound deck. One room features a massive fireplace, built-in bookshelves, and access to the lofty study; the other contains a unique window greenhouse. For the ultimate in privacy, the master bedroom suite possesses a lavish skylit tub. On the lower level are two additional bedrooms, a bath, and a rec room with a bar that opens onto a patio — perfect for outdoor entertaining!

PHOTOGRAPHY BY BETH SINGER

Total Living Area: 3,903 sq. ft.

EYE-CATCHING ANGLES & WINDOWS

This room provides soaring ceilings, dramatic angles, and plenty of natural light. Enjoy the warmth from the wood stove, accentuated by a beautiful stone hearth, while the ceiling fan quietly spins above.

PLEASING STEP-UP TUB

Just off the first floor Master suite, retreat to this private sanctuary, highlighted by a wonderful step-up tub. Soak away the stress of the day and enjoy all the details of this lovely tiled and natural wood room.

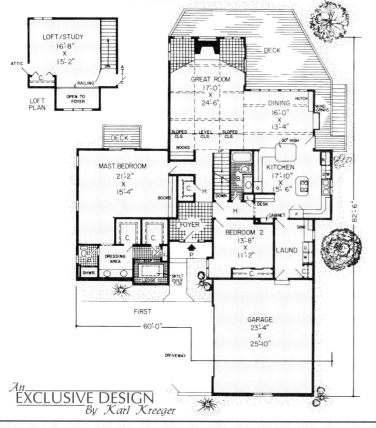

THIS PLAN HAS BEEN MODIFIED TO SUIT INDIVIDUAL TASTES.

DESIGN 10583

★ Main floor	2,367 sq. ft.
★ Basement floor	1,241 sq. ft.
★ Loft	295 sq. ft.
★ Garage	660 sq. ft.
★ Bedrooms	Four
★ Baths	3(Full)
★ Foundation	Basement

REFER TO PRICE CODE F

LOFT/STUDY
16'-8"
X
15'-2"

ATTIC

ATTIC

OPEN TO FOYER

RAILING

LOFT PLAN

DECK

DECK

GREAT ROOM
17'-0"
X
24'-6"

DINING
16'-0"
X
13'-4"

HUTCH

WIND. GRN/HS

SLOPED CLG.   LEVEL CLG.   SLOPED CLG.

30" HIGH

BOOKS

UP

KITCHEN
17'-10"
X
15'-6"

MAST. BEDROOM
21'-2"
X
15'-4"

BOOKS

C.   H.

DOWN

H.

DESK

CABINET

FOYER

BEDROOM 2
13'-8"
X
11'-2"

SINK

LAUND.

C.

C.

DRESSING AREA

SHWR.

SKYLT. OVER TUB

LEDGE

P.

FIRST

60'-0"

82'-6"

GARAGE
23'-4"
X
25'-10"

DRIVEWAY

REC. ROOM
17'-0"
X
25'-6"

PATIO

BEDROOM 3
13'-6"
X
13'-4"

DRIVEWAY

UP

H.

BEDROOM 4
12'-0"
X
14'-10"

MECHANICS GARAGE
21'-2"
X
29'-4"

BAR AREA

LIN.

C.

B.

BSMT.

C.

BASEMENT/LOWER FLOOR

An
EXCLUSIVE DESIGN
By Karl Kreeger

Three Levels of Spacious Living

*T*his passive solar design is suitable for a vacation home or year round living. The rear or southern elevation of the home is highlighted by an abundance of decks and glass. A minimum of windows are found on the north, east and west sides. The basement level has a large shop, storage and recreation areas, plus a bedroom. The first level living room is two steps up from the rest of the first floor, with two stories of glass on its southern wall. An angled wall lends character and interesting decorating ideas to the kitchen/dining area. The master suite occupies the entire second level and contains its own bath, dressing area, walk-in closet, storage nook and private deck.

PHOTOGRAPHY BY JOHN EHRENCLOU

COZY STONE FIREPLACE

Enjoy the impact of this stunning two-story, stone fireplace and soaring ceilings. This living room provides plenty of atmosphere and inspires cozy conversation.

WINDOWS ADD MUCH LIGHT

A full wall of windows adds drama and light to this stunning, open living room. Follow the stairs up to the second floor balcony which looks out over this exciting, naturally lit room.

THIS PLAN HAS BEEN MODIFIED TO SUIT INDIVIDUAL TASTES.

BALCONY

UPPER LIVING ROOM

LANDING

DN

MASTER BEDROOM
18'-0" X 11'-6"

18'-0"

DRESSING

B.

WALK-IN CLO.

STOR.

26'-0"

SECOND FLOOR

*Total Living Area:
2,228 sq. ft.*

DESIGN 10396

★ First floor	886 sq. ft.
★ Second floor	456 sq. ft.
★ Basement floor	886 sq. ft.
★ Bedrooms	Three
★ Baths	3(Full)
★ Foundation	Basement

REFER TO PRICE CODE D

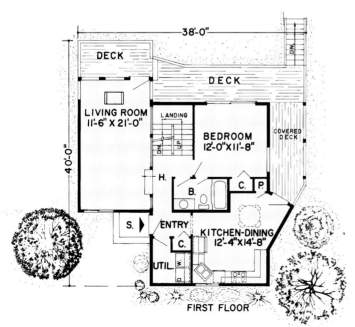

38'-0"

DN

DECK

DECK

LIVING ROOM
11'-6" X 21'-0"

LANDING

DN UP

BEDROOM
12'-0"X11'-8"

COVERED DECK

40'-0"

H.

B.

C.

P.

S.

ENTRY

KITCHEN-DINING
12'-4"X14'-8"

UTIL.

W.

C.

FIRST FLOOR

32'-0"

RECREATION ROOM
11'-10" X 20'-8"

UP

BEDROOM
11'-10"X11'-6"

34'-0"

B.

C.

HW

F.

SHOP & STORAGE
18'-8"X11'-4"

BASEMENT

The Great Outdoors

*T*he first floor living space of this inviting home blends the family room and the dining room together for comfortable family living. The large kitchen shares a preparation/eating bar with the dining room. The ample utility room is designed with a pantry, plus room for a freezer, a washer and a dryer if you so desire. Also on the first floor is the master suite with its two closets and five-piece bath which opens onto a greenhouse. The second floor is highlighted by a loft which overlooks the first floor living area. The two upstairs bedrooms each have double closets and share a four-piece, compartmentalized bath. This plan aims to please in a vacation setting or a year-round environment.

PHOTOGRAPHY BY JOHN EHRENCLOU

DELIGHTFUL EATING AREAS

This open kitchen leads to a variety of eating choices...from a casual dinner at the counter, to a more organized gathering in the dining room. Enjoy the open, beamed ceiling and plenty of natural light from the huge oversized windows.

THIS PLAN HAS BEEN MODIFIED TO SUIT INDIVIDUAL TASTES.

COZY LIVING SPACES

Picture a roaring fire, and plenty of good conversation in this lovely living room. The high, cathedral ceilings and beams add plenty of atmosphere for you and your guests to enjoy.

Total Living Area: 2,015 sq. ft.

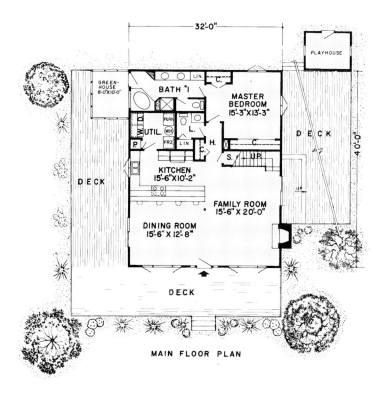

MAIN FLOOR PLAN

- GREEN-HOUSE 8'-0" X 10'-0"
- BATH #1
- MASTER BEDROOM 15'-3" X 13'-3"
- UTIL
- KITCHEN 15'-6" X 10'-2"
- FAMILY ROOM 15'-6" X 20'-0"
- DINING ROOM 15'-6" X 12'-8"
- DECK
- PLAYHOUSE
- 32'-0"
- 40'-0"

DESIGN 10515

★ First floor	1,280 sq. ft.
★ Second floor	735 sq. ft.
★ Greenhouse	80 sq. ft.
★ Playhouse	80 sq. ft.
★ Bedrooms	Three
★ Baths	2(Full)
★ Foundation	Crawl space

REFER TO PRICE CODE C

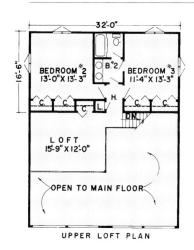

UPPER LOFT PLAN

- BEDROOM #2 13'-0" X 13'-3"
- B #2
- BEDROOM #3 11'-4" X 13'-3"
- LOFT 15'-9" X 12'-0"
- OPEN TO MAIN FLOOR
- 32'-0"
- 16'-6"

Efficient Layout...Relax & Enjoy

*A*lthough rustic in appearance, the interior of this cabin is quiet, modern and comfortable. Small in overall size, it still contains three bedrooms and two baths in addition to a large, two-story living room with exposed beams. As a hunting/fishing lodge or mountain retreat, this compares well.

PHOTOGRAPHY BY STEELE PHOTOGRAPHERS

EFFICIENT KITCHEN TREASURES

This kitchen has everything that you'll need to create your family's meals. The island provides plenty of extra counterspace, and flows into the large living room. This area is sure to be one of the main gathering spots in your home.

EYE-CATCHING ADD-ONS

Enjoy the creative use of add-ons, filled with natural light and entertaining options.

THIS PLAN HAS BEEN MODIFIED TO SUIT INDIVIDUAL TASTES.

Total Living Area: 1,328 sq. ft.

DESIGN 34600

★ First floor	1,013 sq. ft.
★ Second floor	315 sq. ft.
★ Basement	1,013 sq. ft.
★ Bedrooms	Three
★ Baths	2(Full)
★ Foundation	Basement, Slab, Crawl space

REFER TO PRICE CODE A

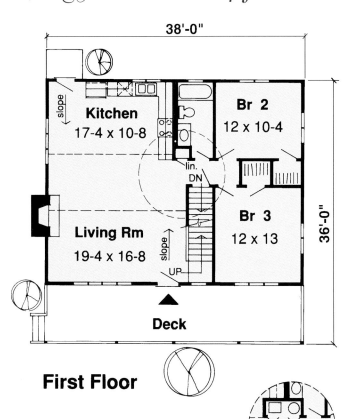

38'-0"

Kitchen
17-4 x 10-8

Br 2
12 x 10-4

slope

lin.

DN

Living Rm
19-4 x 16-8

slope

UP

Br 3
12 x 13

36'-0"

Deck

First Floor

Slab/Crawlspace
Option

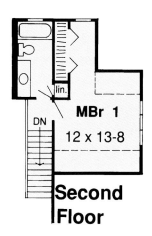

lin.

DN

MBr 1
12 x 13-8

**Second
Floor**

Prize-Winning Solar Home

*T*his cozy solar home took top prize in a nationwide design contest. Inside is a floor plan that's flexible enough to satisfy a wide variety of families and life-styles. The dominant feature of this passive solar system is the 32-foot long greenhouse where the sun's heat is collected, stored and shared with the rest of the house, cutting energy bills in half. This plan offers open spaces and partial ceilings to maximize airflow throughout.

THIS PLAN HAS BEEN MODIFIED TO SUIT INDIVIDUAL TASTES.

PLENTY OF BUILT-INS

This home has a place for everything! The kitchen boasts a convenient pass-thru to the dining room, a built-in wine rack, and plenty of extra closet and cubbie space throughout.

DETAILS ADD IMPACT

This living room looks out onto the greenhouse, creating plenty of conversation and interest. The architectural details of the ceiling, the stairwells, and the greenhouse add plenty of exciting drama.

DESIGN 19863

★ First floor	1.000 sq. ft.
★ Second floor	572 sq. ft.
★ Greenhouse	272 sq. ft.
★ Bedrooms	Three
★ Baths	2(Full)
★ Foundation	Basement

REFER TO PRICE CODE B

BEDRM
13'0''x10'8''

BATH.

KIT
10'3''x11'2''

DEN
13'0''x9'2''

UP

DN

DINING
8'10''x11'2''

ENTRY

LIVING
16'8''x11'2''

WIDTH 42'-8''
DEPTH 32'-5''

GREEN HOUSE
31'4''x8'0''

MAIN LEVEL

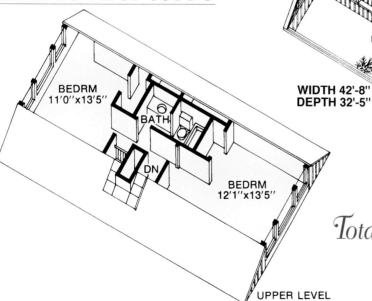

BEDRM
11'0''x13'5''

BATH

DN

BEDRM
12'1''x13'5''

Total Living Area: 1,572 sq. ft.

UPPER LEVEL

Keep It Simple

PHOTOGRAPHY BY JOHN EHRENCLOU

*P*erfect for vacation living, this chalet
beach home features several
worksaving ideas, including a breakfast bar
which divides the living room and kitchen.
The ample living/dining room spills out
onto the attractive 24 foot deck. Four
closeted bedrooms include two upstairs,
favored with balconies and reached by a spiral staircase off the living room. The home
is built on treated pilings, but might also be
constructed on a conventional foundation.

Total Living Area:
1,174 sq. ft.

DESIGN 10054

★ First floor	768 sq. ft.
★ Second floor	406 sq. ft.
★ Bedrooms	Four
★ Baths	1(Full)
★ Foundation	Pilings

REFER TO PRICE CODE A

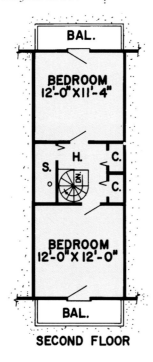

BAL.

BEDROOM
12'-0"X11'-4"

S.   H.   C.

DN.

C.

BEDROOM
12'-0"X12'-0"

BAL.

SECOND FLOOR

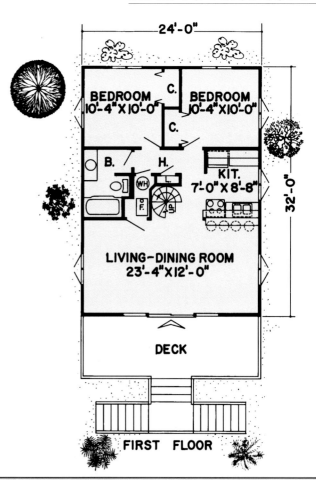

24'-0"

BEDROOM
10'-4"X10'-0"   C.

BEDROOM
10'-4"X10'-0"

C.

B.   H.

WH   KIT.
7'-0"X8'-8"

F.

UP.

32'-0"

LIVING-DINING ROOM
23'-4"X12'-0"

DECK

FIRST FLOOR

THIS PLAN HAS BEEN MODIFIED TO SUIT INDIVIDUAL TASTES.

DESIGN 26111

PHOTOGRAPHY BY JOHN EHRENCLOU

★ First floor	769 sq. ft.
★ Second floor	572 sq. ft.
★ Basement	546 sq. ft.
★ Bedrooms	Three
★ Baths	2(Full)
★ Foundation	Basement

REFER TO PRICE CODE A

*T*he features of this multi-level contemporary home lend character to both the exterior and interior. A wooden deck skirts most of three sides. The variety in the size and shape of doors and windows adds charm. Inside, the living room forms a unique living center. It can be reached from sliding glass doors from the deck or down several steps from the main living level inside. It is overlooked by a low balcony from the entryway and dining room on the lower level and from the second floor landing. Large windows on both the right and the left keep it well lit. Ceilings slope upward two stories. A partial basement is located below the design.

Total Living Area: 1,341 sq. ft.

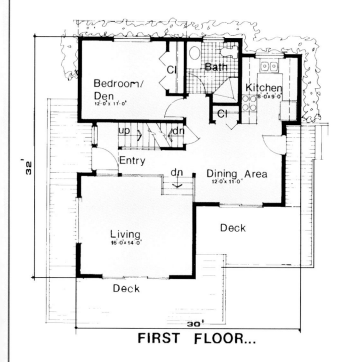

FIRST FLOOR...

SECOND FLOOR...

THIS PLAN HAS BEEN MODIFIED TO SUIT INDIVIDUAL TASTES.

Attractive Elevation

The second level of this home encompasses the master bedroom, master bath, walk-in closet and a loft/study area accented by a fireplace and a private deck. Privacy for the owner is assured. On the first floor, the entrance into the living room provides a terrific first impression. A massive fireplace accents the room. Adjoining the living room is the formal dining room which opens onto a rear deck. For informal meals there is convenient sitting at the breakfast bar extending from the efficient kitchen. Two additional bedrooms share the full hall bath. No materials list is available for this plan.

DESIGN 94301

★ First floor	1,145 sq. ft.
★ Second floor	/26 sq. ft.
★ Garage	433 sq. ft.
★ Bedrooms	Three
★ Baths	2(Full)
★ Foundation	Crawl space

REFER TO PRICE CODE C

Total Living Area: 1,871 sq. ft.

2ND FLOOR

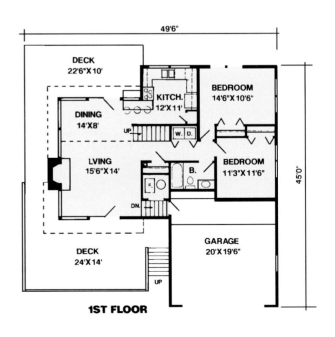

1ST FLOOR

An EXCLUSIVE DESIGN *By Marshall Associates*

-14-

DESIGN 94305

★ First floor	680 sq. ft.
★ Second floor	345 sq. ft.
★ Garage	357 sq. ft.
★ Bedrooms	Two
★ Baths	2(Full)
★ Foundation	Crawl space

REFER TO PRICE CODE A

An
EXCLUSIVE DESIGN
By Marshall Associates

This plan offers a contemporary look on an A-frame design. The spa deck pampers you while you enjoy the surrounding vistas. A second deck is located off of the living room. A cozy fireplace adds warmth and atmosphere, enhancing the entire open living area of the living room and kitchen. A peninsula counter/eating bar, double sink and ample storage and workspace are featured in the kitchen. The first floor bedroom is located in close proximity to the three quarter bath in the hall. A spacious master suite is located on the second floor providing the owner the luxury of privacy. No materials list is available for this plan.

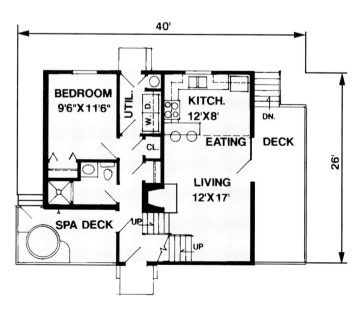

LOWER/MID LEVELS

UPPER LEVEL

Total Living Area: 1,025 sq. ft.

Enticing Angles

*A*n attractive elevation to be placed in your dream environment, perhaps perched on a mountainside or by a lake. A deck expands living space outdoors. The open layout between the dining and living room is accented by a central fireplace. An efficient U-shaped kitchen includes a corner double sink surrounded by three windows providing a view. Two bedrooms are included, one with a private bath and a walk-in closet.

DESIGN 94300

★ Main floor	950 sq. ft.
★ Bedrooms	Two
★ Baths	2(Full)
★ Foundation	Crawl space

REFER TO PRICE CODE A

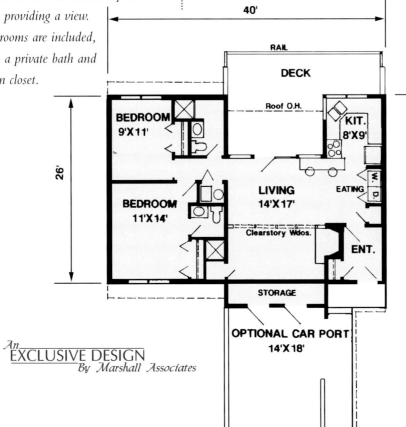

40'

RAIL

DECK

Roof O.H.

BEDROOM
9'X11'

KIT.
8'X9'

26'

LIVING
14'X17'

EATING

W.
D.

BEDROOM
11'X14'

Clearstory Wdos.

ENT.

53'

STORAGE

OPTIONAL CAR PORT
14'X18'

Total Living Area:
950 sq. ft.

An
EXCLUSIVE DESIGN
By Marshall Associates

DESIGN 94306

★ First floor	598 sq. ft.
★ Second floor	414 sq. ft.
★ Bedrooms	Three
★ Baths	2(Full)
★ Foundation	Crawl space

REFER TO PRICE CODE A

An
EXCLUSIVE DESIGN
By Marshall Associates

Total Living Area:
1,012 sq. ft.

Sitting in the living room of this home you can look out over your beautiful surroundings through a wall of glass. Through the glass doors you can be one with nature lounging on the wooden deck. A center fireplace in the middle of the living/dining area gives warmth and a coziness to the atmosphere. The efficient kitchen includes access to the outside through a side door and a convenient closet as well as ample cabinet and work space. The first floor bedroom is in close proximity to the full hall bath. The second floor includes the private master suite, a laundry center and a loft bedroom. The master suite is further enhanced by a private deck. No materials list is available for this plan.

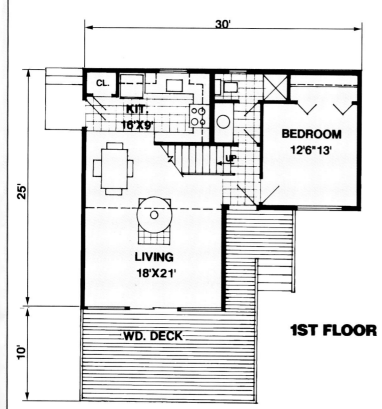

30'

CL.

KIT.
16'X9'

BEDROOM
12'6"13'

UP

25'

LIVING
18'X21'

10'

WD. DECK

1ST FLOOR

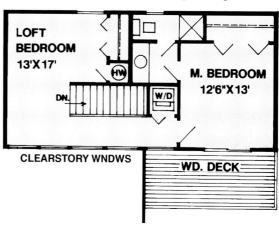

LOFT
BEDROOM
13'X17'

HW

DN.

W/D

M. BEDROOM
12'6"X13'

CLEARSTORY WNDWS

WD. DECK

2ND FLOOR

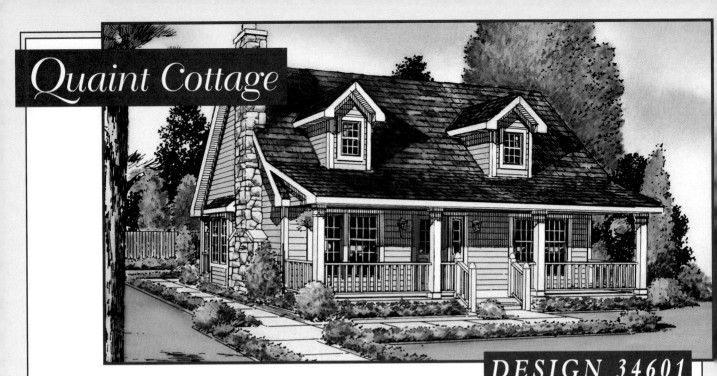

Quaint Cottage

A large front porch is always an old-fashioned welcome to any home. This Cape provides such a welcome. Once inside the home, the vaulted ceiling and grand fireplace of the living room add to the character of this house. The efficient kitchen has a double sink and a peninsula counter that may double as an eating bar. A laundry center is conveniently located in the full bath. Two of the three bedrooms are located on the first floor. The second floor provides the privacy the master suite deserves. Sloping ceilings, a walk-in closet and a private master bath give the owner of this home a private retreat on the second floor. No materials is list available for this plan.

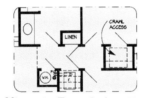

Alternate Foundation Plan

DESIGN 34601

★ First floor	1,007 sq. ft.
★ Second floor	408 sq. ft.
★ Basement	1,007 sq. ft.
★ Bedrooms	Three
★ Baths	2(Full)
★ Foundation	Basement, Slab, Crawl space

REFER TO PRICE CODE A

Total Living Area: 1,415 sq. ft.

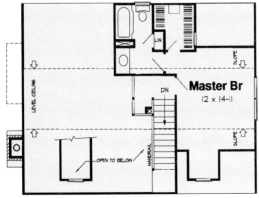

SECOND FLOOR

FIRST FLOOR

For Today & Tomorrow

DESIGN 34043

★ First floor	1,583 sq. ft.
★ Basement	1,583 sq. ft.
★ Garage	484 sq. ft.
★ Bedrooms	Three
★ Baths	2(Full)
★ Foundation	Basement, Slab, Crawl space

REFER TO PRICE CODE B

*T*his convenient, one-level plan is perfect for the modern family with a taste for classic design. Traditional Victorian touches in this three-bedroom beauty include a romantic, railed porch and an intriguing breakfast tower just off the kitchen. You will love the step-saving arrangement of the kitchen between the breakfast and formal dining rooms. Enjoy the wide-open living room with sliders out to a rear deck, and the handsome master suite with its skylit, compartmentalized bath. Notice the convenient laundry location on the bedroom hall.

An
EXCLUSIVE DESIGN
By Karl Kreeger

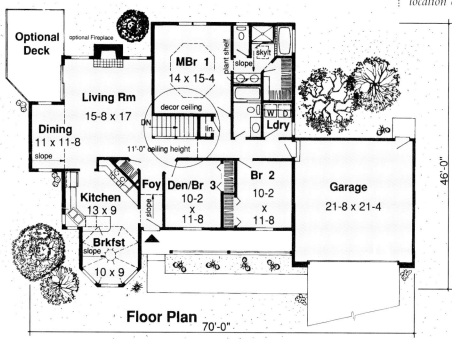

Floor Plan

Slab/Crawlspace Option

Total Living Area:
1,583 sq. ft.

Perfect Vacation Home

*F*amily vacations are memories in the making. This home will help to make those precious times. Three bedrooms give private space to all. If you don't have a large family, make one bedroom into a study or maybe a hobby room, the possibilities are endless. The living room, with a fireplace, is large and open and can extend your living area out of the home with access to two decks. The efficient kitchen opens to the dining area. The master bedroom features a private bath with corner tub. There are also two closets in this room. Looking forward to retirement? This home may be what you are looking for. All the living area is on one floor, yet it is spacious and layed out with convenience in mind.

Total Living Area: 1,127 sq. ft.

Basement Option

DESIGN 24311

★ Main floor	1,127 sq. ft.
★ Bedrooms	Three
★ Baths	2(Full)
★ Foundation	Basement, Crawl space

REFER TO PRICE CODE A

An EXCLUSIVE DESIGN *By Marshall Associates*

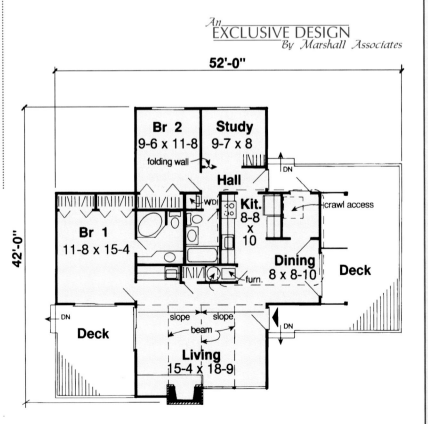

DESIGN 26110

★ First floor	902 sq. ft.
★ Second floor	567 sq. ft.
★ Bedrooms	Three
★ Baths	1(Full), 1(Half)
★ Foundation	Basement

REFER TO PRICE CODE A

*N*umerous south-facing glass doors and windows, skylights and a greenhouse clue the exterior viewer to this passive solar contemporary design. For minimum heat loss, 2x6 studs for R-19 insulation are used in exterior walls, and R-33 insulation is used in all sloping ceilings. The living room employs a concrete slab floor for solar gain. Basement space is located under the kitchen, dining room, lower bedroom and den. A northern entrance through a vestibule and French doors channels you upward to the first floor living area. A unique feature on this level is the skylit living room ceiling which slants two stories. Second story rooms are lit by clerestory windows. Two balconies are on this level: an exterior one off the bedroom and an interior one overlooking the living room.

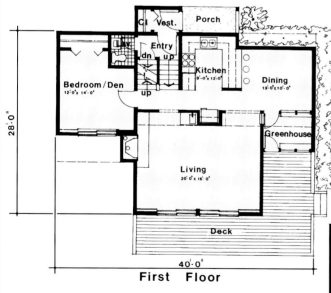

First Floor

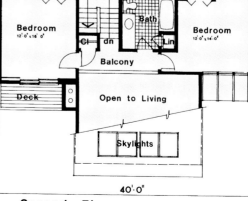

Second Floor

Total Living Area:
1,469 sq. ft.

Three Spacious Levels

An
EXCLUSIVE DESIGN
By Marshall Associates

This home is a vacation haven with views from every room whether it is situated on a lake or a mountaintop. The main floor features a living room and dining room split by a fireplace. The kitchen flows into the dining room and is gracefully separated by a bar. There is a bedroom and a full bath on the main floor. The second floor has a bedroom or library loft, with clerestory windows, which opens above the living room. The master bedroom and bath are also on the top floor. The lower floor has a large recreation room with a whirlpool tub and a bar, a laundry room and a garage. This home has large decks and windows on one entire side.

Total Living Area: 1,680 sq. ft.

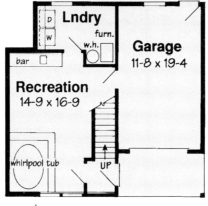

Lndry
D
W
bar
furn.
w.h.
Garage
11-8 x 19-4
Recreation
14-9 x 16-9
whirlpool tub
UP

Lower Floor

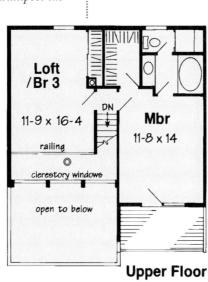

Loft /Br 3
11-9 x 16-4
DN
railing
clerestory windows
open to below
Mbr
11-8 x 14

Upper Floor

DESIGN 24319

★ Main floor	728 sq. ft.
★ Upper floor	573 sq. ft.
★ Lower floor	379 sq. ft.
★ Garage	240 sq. ft.
★ Bedrooms	Three
★ Baths	2(Full)
★ Foundation	Basement

REFER TO PRICE CODE B

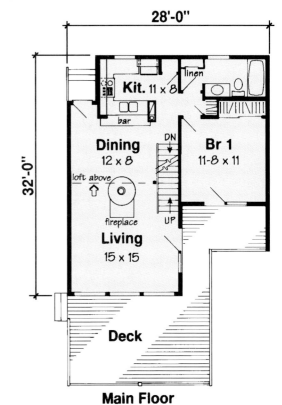

28'-0"
32'-0"
linen
Kit. 11 x 8
bar
Dining 12 x 8
loft above
DN
Br 1 11-8 x 11
fireplace
UP
Living 15 x 15
Deck

Main Floor

DESIGN 20501

★ First floor — 1,316 sq. ft.

★ Second floor — 592 sq. ft.

★ Bedrooms — Three

★ Baths — 2(Full)

★ Foundation — Basement, Crawl space

REFER TO PRICE CODE C

Total Living Area: 1,908 sq. ft.

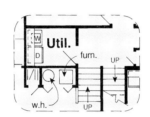

Pier/ Crawl Space Option

*Y*our hillside lot is no problem if you choose this spectacular, multi-level sun-catcher. Window walls combine with sliders to unite active areas with a huge outdoor deck. Interior spaces flow together for an open feeling that's accentuated by the sloping ceilings and towering fireplace in the living room. Thanks to the island kitchen, even the cook can stay involved in the action. Walk up a short flight to reach the laundry room, a full bath, and two bedrooms, each with a walk-in closet. Up a separate staircase, you'll find the master suite, truly a private retreat complete with a garden spa, abundant closets, and balcony.

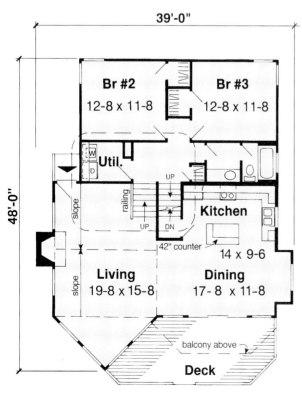

First Floor

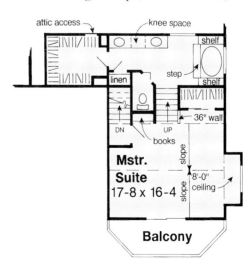

Second Floor

Detailed Charmer

Walk past the charming front porch, in through the foyer and you'll be struck by the exciting, spacious living room. Complete with high sloping ceilings and a beautiful fireplace flanked by large windows. The large master bedroom shows off a full wall of closet space, its own private bath, and an extraordinary decorative ceiling. Just down the hall are two more bedrooms and another full bath. Take advantage of the accessibility off the foyer and turn one of these rooms into a private den or office space. The dining room provides a feast for your eyes with its decorative ceiling details, and a full slider out to the deck. Along with great counter space, the kitchen includes a double sink and an attractive bump-out window. The adjacent laundry room, optional expanded pantry, and a two-car garage make this Ranch a charmer.

DESIGN 20161

★ Main floor	1,307 sq. ft.
★ Basement	1,298 sq. ft.
★ Garage	462 sq. ft.
★ Bedrooms	Three
★ Baths	2(Full)
★ Foundation	Basement, Slab, Crawl space

REFER TO PRICE CODE A

An
EXCLUSIVE DESIGN
By Karl Kreeger

Total Living Area:
1,307 sq. ft.

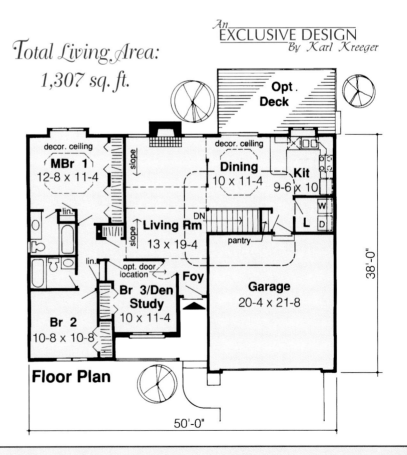

Floor Plan

Slab/Crawl Space Option

Attractive Stone Detailing

DESIGN 34029

★ First floor	1,698 sq. ft.
★ Garage	484 sq. ft.
★ Bedrooms	Three
★ Baths	2(Full)
★ Foundation	Basement, Slab, Crawl space

REFER TO PRICE CODE B

An
EXCLUSIVE DESIGN
By Karl Kreeger

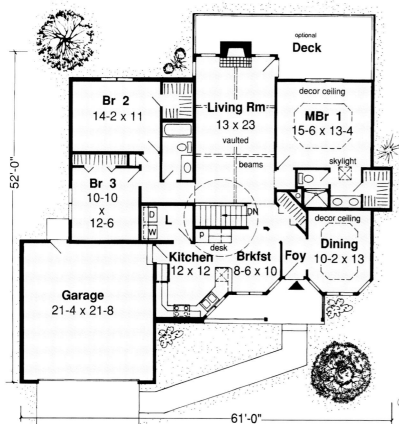

optional
Deck

decor ceiling

Br 2
14-2 x 11

Living Rm
13 x 23
vaulted

MBr 1
15-6 x 13-4

beams

skylight

Br 3
10-10
x
12-6

D L
W

DN

p
desk

decor ceiling

Dining
10-2 x 13

Kitchen
12 x 12

Brkfst
8-6 x 10

Foy

Garage
21-4 x 21-8

52'-0"

61'-0"

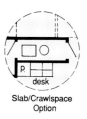

p
desk

Slab/Crawlspace
Option

*K*eep dry during the rainy season under the covered porch entryway of this gorgeous home. A foyer separates the dining room with a decorative ceiling from the breakfast area and the kitchen. Off the kitchen is the laundry room, conveniently located. The living room features a vaulted beamed ceiling and a fireplace. A full bath is located between the living room and two bedrooms, both with large closet. On the other side of the living room is the master bedroom. The master bedroom has a decorative ceiling, and a skylight above the entrance of its private bath. The double-vanitied bathroom features a large walk-in closet. For those who enjoy outdoor living, an optional deck is offered, accessible through sliding glass doors off of this wonderful master bedroom.

Total Living Area: 1,698 sq. ft.

Everything You Need

S tep into the sunwashed foyer of this contemporary beauty, and you'll be faced with a choice. You can walk downstairs into a huge, fireplaced rec room with built-in bar and adjoining patio. Or, you can ascend the stairs to a massive living room with sloping ceilings, a tiled fireplace, and a commanding view of the backyard. Sharing the view, the breakfast nook with sunny bay opens to an outdoor deck. The adjoining kitchen is just steps away from the formal dining room, which features recessed ceilings and overlooks the foyer. You'll also find the master suite on this level, just past the powder room off the living room. Three more bedrooms and a full bath are located on the lower level.

An
EXCLUSIVE DESIGN
By Karl Kreeger

Total Living Area:
2,477 sq. ft.

DESIGN 20095

★ Upper floor	1,448 sq. ft.
★ Lower floor	1,029 sq. ft.
★ Garage	504 sq. ft.
★ Bedrooms	Four
★ Baths	2(Full),1(Half)
★ Foundation	Crawl space

REFER TO PRICE CODE D

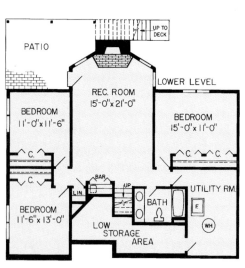

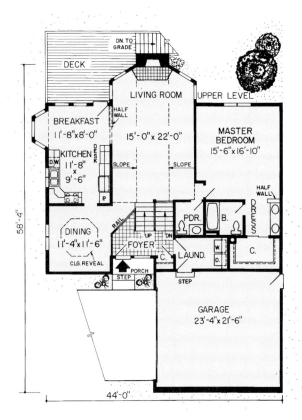

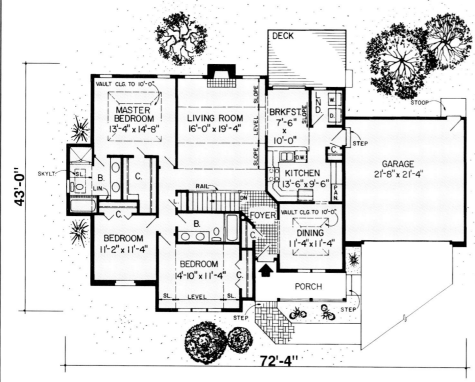

Abundant Windows

DESIGN 20100

★ First floor	1,737 sq. ft.
★ Basement	1,727 sq. ft.
★ Garage	484 sq. ft.
★ Bedrooms	Three
★ Baths	2(Full)
★ Foundation	Basement, Slab, Crawl space

REFER TO PRICE CODE B

An
EXCLUSIVE DESIGN
By Karl Kreeger

*S*tacked windows fill the wall in the front bedroom of this one-level home, creating an attractive facade and a sunny atmosphere inside. Around the corner, two more bedrooms and two full baths complete the bedroom wing, set apart for bedtime quiet. Notice the elegant vaulted-ceiling in the master bedroom, the master tub and shower illuminated by a skylight, and the double vanities in both baths. Active areas enjoy a spacious feeling. Look at the high, sloping ceilings in the fireplaced living room, the sliders that unite the breakfast room and kitchen with an adjoining deck, and the vaulted-ceilings in the formal dining room off the foyer.

Total Living Area:
1,737 sq. ft.

PRICE CODE A

DESIGN 20164

Total Living Area: 1,456 sq. ft.

*H*ere's a pretty, one-level home designed for carefree living. The central foyer divides active and quiet areas. Step back to a fireplaced living room with dramatic, towering ceilings and a panoramic view of the backyard. The adjoining dining room features a sloping ceiling crowned by a plant shelf, and sliders to an outdoor deck. Just across the counter, a handy, U-shaped kitchen features abundant cabinets, a window over the sink overlooking the deck, and a walk-in pantry. You'll find three bedrooms tucked off the foyer. Front bedrooms share a handy full bath, but the master suite boasts its own private bath with both shower and tub, a room-sized walk-in closet, and a bump-out window that adds light and space.

An EXCLUSIVE DESIGN *By Karl Kreeger*

Optional Deck

Dining 10 x 12

plant shelf

Living 13-2 x 19-4

slope

MBr 1 11-8 x 14 decor. ceiling

Kit 9-4 x 13-4

W D

DN

pantry

Foyer

Garage 19-4 x 23-8

Den/Br 3 10-5 x 11-6

Br 2 10-5 x 10-6

Floor Plan

44'-0"

50'-0"

Main area — 1,456 sq. ft.
Basement — 1,448 sq. ft.
Garage — 452 sq. ft.
Bedrooms — Three
Bathrooms — 2(Full)
Foundation — Basement, Slab Crawl space

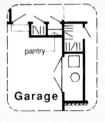

pantry

Garage

Slab/Crawl Space Option

DESIGN 84058

Total Living Area: 1,298 sq. ft.

*E*fficient use of living space creates a spacious feeling in this home perfect for a lakeside location. The living/dining area occupies more than half of the lower level while the balcony overlooking the living area affords an expansive illusion. The central chimney will accommodate a built-in fireplace. The fully-equipped bath adjoins two liberal bedrooms on the upper level. Available in slab, crawl, and basement foundation options. No materials list available for this plan.

First floor — 779 sq. ft.
Second floor — 519 sq. ft.
Bedrooms — Three
Bathrooms — 2(Full)
Foundation — Basement, Slab, Crawl space

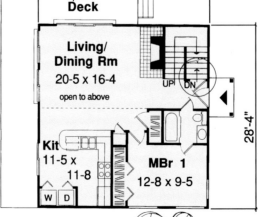

27'-6"

optional Deck

Living/ Dining Rm 20-5 x 16-4

open to above

UP DN

Kit 11-5 x 11-8

W D

MBr 1 12-8 x 9-5

28'-4"

First Floor

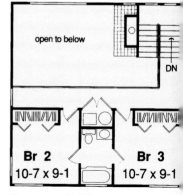

open to below

DN

Br 2 10-7 x 9-1

Br 3 10-7 x 9-1

Second Floor

PRICE CODE A

DESIGN 26112

*W*ood adds its warmth to the contemporary features of this solar design. Generous use of southern glass doors and windows, an air-lock entry, skylights and a living room fireplace reduce energy needs. R-26 insulation is used for floors and sloping ceilings. Decking rims the front of the home and gives access through sliding glass doors to a bedroom/den area and living room. The dining room lies up several steps from the living room and is separated from it by a half-wall. The dining room flows into the kitchen through an eating bar. A second floor landing balcony overlooks the living room. Two bedrooms, one with its own private deck, and a full bath finish the second level.

First floor — 911 sq. ft.
Second floor — 576 sq. ft.
Basement — 911 sq. ft.
Bedrooms — Three
Bathrooms — 1 (Full), 1 (Half)
Foundation — Basement

Total Living Area: 1,487 sq. ft.

SECOND FLOOR

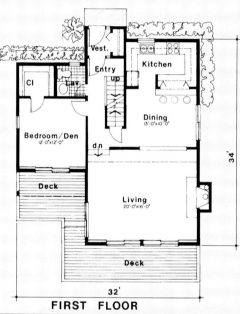

FIRST FLOOR

PRICE CODE A

Easy Living Plan

Sophisticated Chalet Design

DESIGN 9964

PRICE CODE A

Total Living Area: 1,353 sq. ft.

*T*his romantic chalet design would be equally appealing along an ocean beach or mountain stream. Restful log fires will add atmosphere in the sizable recreation room bordering the patio of this chalet. Upstairs, another fireplace warms the living and dining rooms which are accessible to the large wooden sun deck. Four bedrooms and two baths are outlined. The home is completely insulated for year round convenience and contains washer and dryer space.

First floor — 896 sq. ft.
Second floor — 457 sq. ft.
Basement — 864 sq. ft.
Bedrooms — Four
Bathrooms — 2(Full)
Foundation — Basement

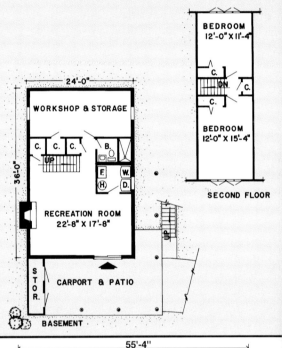

DESIGN 24250

*T*he design of this home allows for plenty of living space. This home makes use of custom, volume ceilings. The living room offers a sunk-in environment. The vaulted ceiling and fireplace give this room drama. The oversized windows framing the fireplace enhance the drama with natural light. The kitchen features a center island and eating nook. The formal dining room adjoins the kitchen allowing for easy entertaining. The spacious master suite enjoys a vaulted ceiling. Cozy, comfortable, and peaceful are the feelings you get as you curl up on the window seat on a rainy afternoon to read your book. The secondary bedrooms also have custom ceiling treatments and large windows that view the front porch.

Main floor — 1,700 sq. ft.
Bedrooms — Three
Bathrooms — 2(Full)
Foundation — Basement, Crawl space

Total Living Area: 1,700 sq. ft.

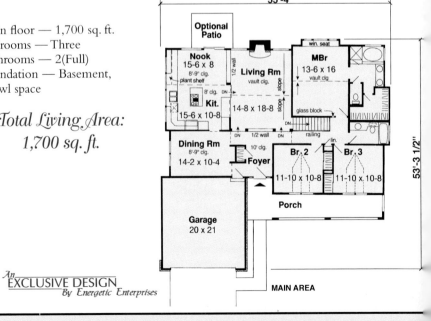

An EXCLUSIVE DESIGN *By Energetic Enterprises*

-30-

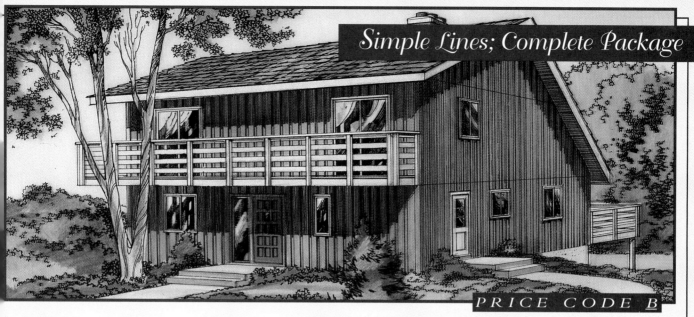

Simple Lines; Complete Package

PRICE CODE B

Total Living Area: 1,600 sq. ft.

DESIGN 10328

*E*quipped with fireplace and sliding glass doors to the bordering deck, the two-story living room creates a sizeable and airy center for family activity. A well-planned traffic pattern connects the dining area, kitchen, laundry niche and bath. Closets are plentiful, and a total of three 15-foot bedrooms are shown. A balcony overlooking the open living room is featured on the second floor.

First floor — 1,024 sq. ft.
Second floor — 576 sq. ft.
Basement — 1,024 sq. ft.
Bedrooms — Three
Bathrooms — 2(Full)
Foundation — Basement

Easy Living Plan

PRICE CODE B

Efficient Ranch Design

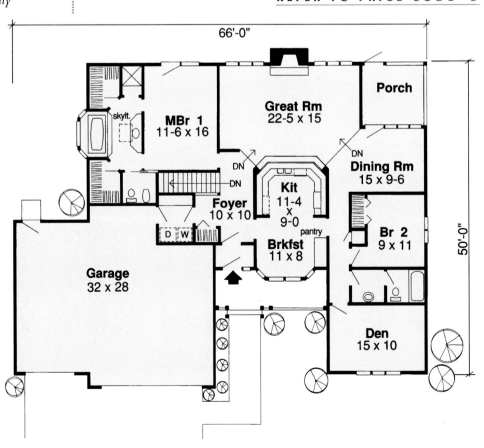

*T*his Ranch home features a large sunken Great room, centralized with a cozy fireplace. The master bedroom has an unforgettable bathroom with a super skylight. The huge three-car plus garage can include a work area for the family carpenter. In the center of this home, a kitchen includes an eating nook for family gatherings. The porch at the rear of the house has easy access from the dining room. One other bedroom and a den, which can easily be converted to a bedroom, are on the opposite side of the house from the master bedroom.

Total Living Area: 1,738 sq. ft.

DESIGN 10839

★ First floor	1,738 sq. ft.
★ Basement	1,083 sq. ft.
★ Garage	796 sq. ft.
★ Bedrooms	Two
★ Baths	2(Full)
★ Foundation	Basement, Slab, Crawl space

REFER TO PRICE CODE B

PRICE CODE B

A-FRAME UPDATE

No. 90844

■ This plan features:

— Three bedrooms

— Two full and one half baths

■ A wrap-around deck adding outdoor living space

■ Two-story glass walls in the Dining Room and Living Room

■ A Master Bedroom with a private half-bath

■ An open loft with an expansive bedroom having its own private deck and full bath

FIRST FLOOR — 1,086 SQ. FT.
SECOND FLOOR — 466 SQ. FT.
BASEMENT — 1,080 SQ. FT.

TOTAL LIVING AREA:
1,552 SQ. FT.

An
EXCLUSIVE DESIGN
By Westhome Planners, Ltd.

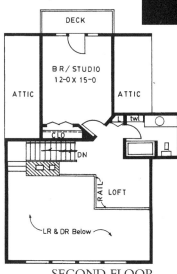

SECOND FLOOR

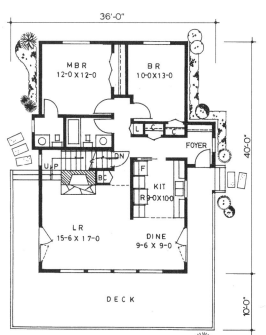

FIRST FLOOR

PRICE CODE A

Built for a View

No. 91722

- This plan features:
— Three bedrooms
— One full bath

- A double-sided fireplace with a tile hearth, separating the Living Room and Kitchen areas, complimented by a wall of windows

- An efficient U-shaped Kitchen with an open cooktop counter and adjoining Utility area

- Two bedrooms on the first floor with large closets sharing a full hall bath

- A private bedroom and extensive storage space on the second floor

First floor — 972 sq. ft.
Second — 277 sq. ft.
Width — 24'-0"
Depth — 42'-0"

Total living area:
1,249 sq. ft.

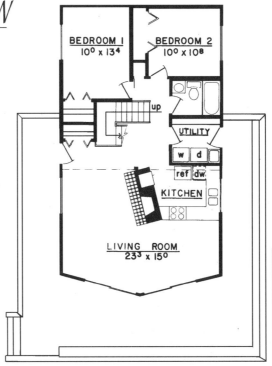

FIRST FLOOR PLAN

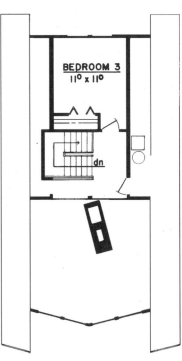

PRICE CODE A

VACATION COTTAGE

An EXCLUSIVE DESIGN
By Westhome Planners, Ltd.

No. 90821

■ This plan features:

— Two bedrooms

— One full bath

■ An economical, neat and simple design

■ Two picture windows in the Living/Dining Room

■ An efficient Kitchen design

■ A large, cozy loft bedroom flanked by big storage rooms

FIRST FLOOR — 616 SQ. FT.
LOFT — 180 SQ. FT.
WIDTH — 22'-0"
DEPTH — 28'-0"

TOTAL LIVING AREA:
796 SQ. FT.

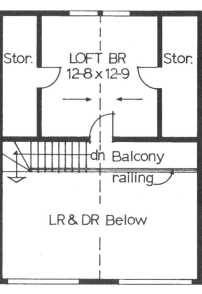

LOFT

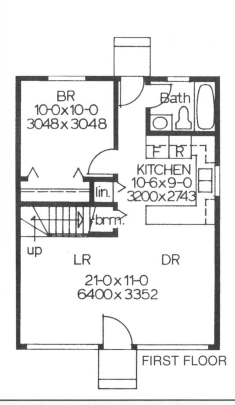

FIRST FLOOR

PRICE CODE A

BEDROOM SLIDERS OPEN ONTO WOODEN DECK

No. 10220

- This plan features:
- — Two bedrooms
- — One full bath
- A fifty foot deck setting the stage for a relaxing lifestyle encouraged by this home
- A simple, yet complete floor plan centering around the large Family Area, warmed by a prefab fireplace and having sliders to the deck
- An efficient L-shaped Kitchen that includes a double sink with a window above, and direct access to the rear yard and the Laundry Room
- Two bedrooms privately located, each outfitted with sliding doors to the deck and a large window for plenty of light

MAIN AREA — 888 SQ. FT.

TOTAL LIVING AREA:
888 SQ. FT.

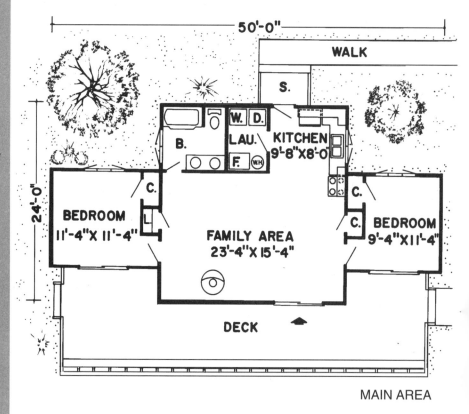

MAIN AREA

PRICE CODE B

UNUSUAL ANGLES ADD STYLE

No. 92804

■ This plan features:

— Three bedrooms

— Two full baths

■ A wooden Deck providing entrance and expanding living space

■ A fireplace surrounded by windows in the two-story Living Room

■ An efficient Kitchen/Dining Area with angled windows

■ Two first floor bedrooms sharing a full hall bath

■ A unique Master Bedroom suite with a spa area, a balcony and a private bath

■ A pole, slab or crawl space foundation allows for varied building sites

FIRST FLOOR — 1,051 SQ. FT.
SECOND FLOOR — 635 SQ. FT.

TOTAL LIVING AREA:
1,686 SQ. FT.

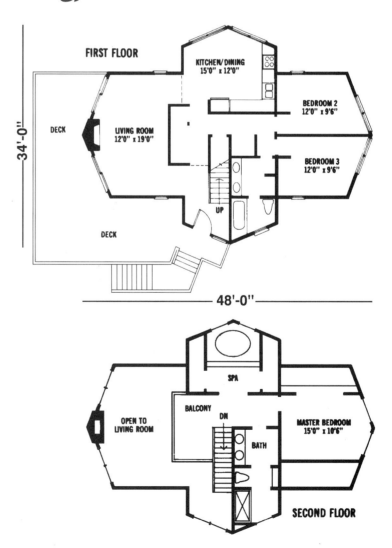

FIRST FLOOR

KITCHEN/DINING
15'0" x 12'0"

BEDROOM 2
12'0" x 9'6"

BEDROOM 3
12'0" x 9'6"

DECK

LIVING ROOM
12'0" x 19'0"

UP

DECK

34'-0"

48'-0"

SPA

BALCONY

DN

OPEN TO LIVING ROOM

MASTER BEDROOM
15'0" x 10'6"

BATH

SECOND FLOOR

PRICE CODE A

WINDOW DESIGN HIGHLIGHTS PLAN

No. 90348

■ This plan features:

— Two bedrooms plus loft

— Two full baths

■ An airy Living Room with glass on three sides and a fireplace tucked into corner

■ An efficient Kitchen serving the Living and Dining Rooms easily

■ First floor Bedrooms featuring a private bath and a walk-in closet connected to Storage area

■ A landing staircase leading to a second bedroom with a walk-in closet, a Laundry and a full Bath

■ A ladder to top-of-the-tower Loft with loads of light and multiple uses

FIRST FLOOR — 729 SQ. FT.
SECOND FLOOR — 420 SQ. FT.
WIDTH — 42'-0"
DEPTH — 32'-8"

TOTAL LIVING AREA:
1,149 SQ. FT.

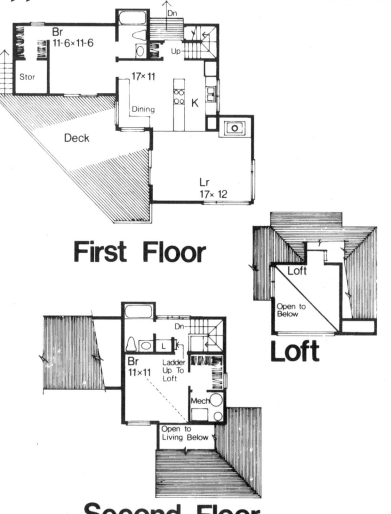

First Floor

Loft

Second Floor

PRICE CODE C

EXTERIOR HIGHLIGHTED BY MANY DECKS

No. 90629

- ■ This plan features:
  - — Three bedrooms
  - — Three full and one half baths
- ■ All rooms with outdoor decks
- ■ A Living Room with a heat-circulating fireplace
- ■ A Kitchen with ample counter and cabinet space and easy access to the Dining Room and outdoor dining area
- ■ A Master Bedroom with a heat-circulating fireplace, plush Master Bath and a walk-in closet
- ■ A basement foundation only

FIRST FLOOR — 1,001 SQ. FT.
SECOND FLOOR — 712 SQ. FT.
LOWER FLOOR — 463 SQ. FT.

**TOTAL LIVING AREA:
2,176 SQ. FT.**

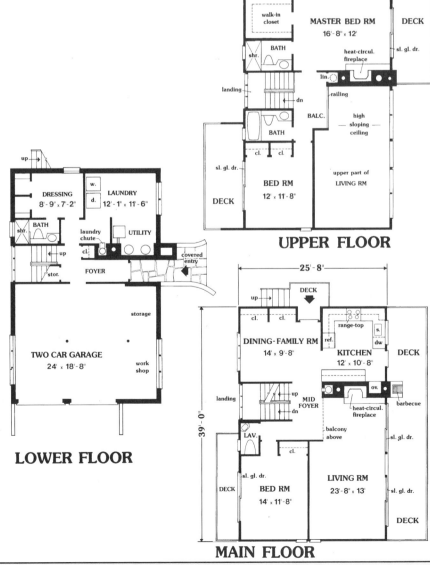

UPPER FLOOR

LOWER FLOOR

MAIN FLOOR

PRICE CODE A

THREE BEDROOM A-FRAME

No. 90995

- This plan features:
- — Three bedrooms
- — One full bath
- A wrap-around Deck providing panoramic views and access to the Dining/Living room area through French doors
- An spacious Living room/Dining area with a glass wall and a vaulted ceiling that opens to the Kitchen
- An well-equipped Kitchen with a serving island, opening to the Dining and Living rooms
- A Mud Room entrance with a large closet, a laundry, and a built-in bench
- Two first floor bedrooms sharing a shower bath
- A large Master Bedroom with French doors to a private Sundeck

FIRST FLOOR — 768 SQ. FT.
SECOND FLOOR — 243 SQ. FT.

TOTAL LIVING AREA:
1,011 SQ. FT.

An
EXCLUSIVE DESIGN
By Westhome Planners, Ltd.

WIDTH — 32'-0"
DEPTH — 46'-0"

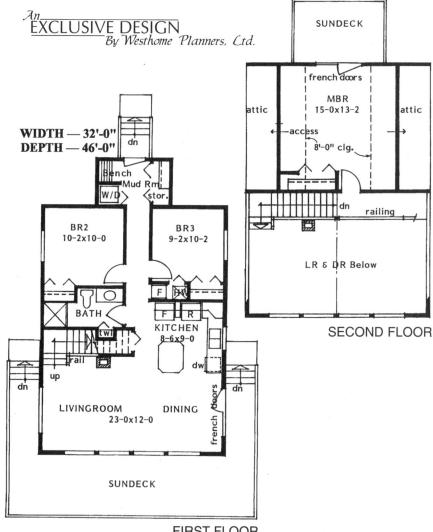

SECOND FLOOR

FIRST FLOOR

PRICE CODE A

RUSTIC CHARM IN A COMFORTABLE COTTAGE

No. 90855

■ This plan features:

— Two bedrooms

— One full and one half baths

■ An expansive two-level Sundeck across the front of the home, providing ample outdoor living

■ A vaulted ceiling with skylights and a fieldstone fireplace surrounded by glass accentuating the Living/Dining Room area

■ An open, L-shaped Kitchen with an eating Nook, a built-in pantry and a broom closet

■ A Master Bedroom with ample closet space, a half bath, and a sliding glass door to deck

■ A second bedroom adjoins a full hall bath with a laundry

MAIN FLOOR — 1,186 SQ. FT.
WIDTH — 41'-0"
DEPTH — 40'-0"

TOTAL LIVING AREA:
1,186 SQ. FT.

An EXCLUSIVE DESIGN
By Westhome Planners, Ltd.

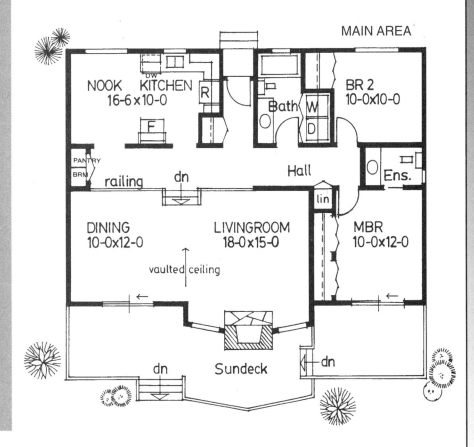

MAIN AREA

NOOK   KITCHEN
16-6 x 10-0

BR 2
10-0x10-0

Bath

PANTRY
BRM

railing   dn

Hall

Ens.

lin

DINING
10-0x12-0

LIVINGROOM
18-0x15-0

MBR
10-0x12-0

vaulted ceiling

dn   Sundeck   dn

PRICE CODE A

NO WASTED SPACE

No. 90412

■ This plan features:

— Three bedrooms

— Two full baths

■ A centrally located Great Room with a cathedral ceiling, exposed wood beams, and large areas of fixed glass

■ The Living and Dining areas separated by a massive stone fireplace

■ A secluded Master Suite with a walk-in closet and private Master Bath

■ An efficient Kitchen with a convenient laundry area

■ An optional basement, slab or crawl space foundation — please specify when ordering

MAIN AREA — 1,454 SQ. FT.

TOTAL LIVING AREA: 1,454 SQ. FT.

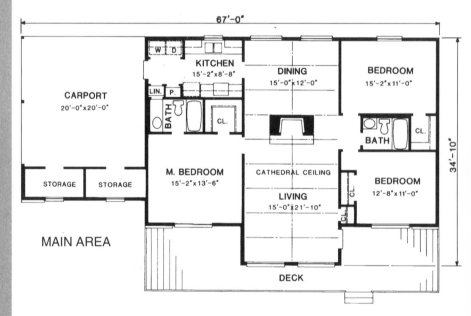

PRICE CODE A

CABIN IN THE COUNTRY

No. 90433

■ This plan features:

— Two bedrooms

— One full and one half baths

■ A screened porch for enjoyment of your outdoor surroundings

■ A combination Living and Dining area with cozy fireplace for added warmth

■ An efficiently laid out Kitchen with a built-in pantry

■ Two large bedrooms located at the rear of the home

■ An optional slab or crawl space foundation — please specify when ordering

FIRST FLOOR — 928 SQ. FT.
SCREENED PORCH — 230 SQ. FT.
STORAGE — 14 SQ. FT.

TOTAL LIVING AREA:
928 SQ. FT.

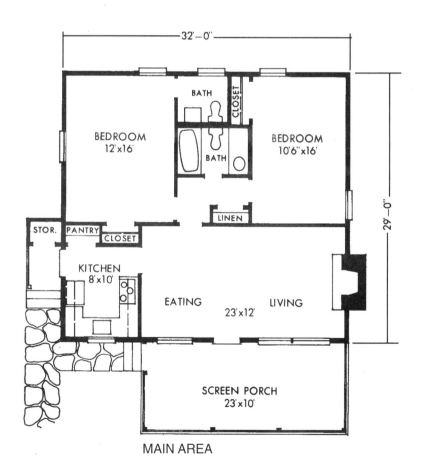

MAIN AREA

PRICE CODE A

YEAR ROUND LEISURE

No. 90630

■ This plan features:

— Three bedrooms

— Two full baths

■ A cathedral ceiling with exposed beams and a stone wall with heat-circulating fireplace in the Living Room

■ Three sliding glass doors leading from the Living Room to a large deck

■ A built-in Dining area that separates the Kitchen from the far end of the Living Room

■ A Master Suite with his and her closets and a private bath

■ Two additional bedrooms, one double sized, sharing a full hall bath

■ A crawl space foundation only

FIRST FLOOR — 1,207 SQ. FT.

TOTAL LIVING AREA:
1,207 SQ. FT.

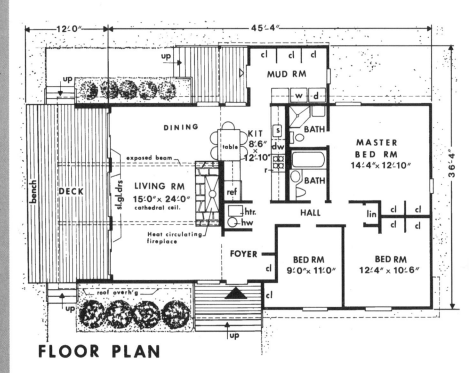

FLOOR PLAN

PRICE CODE A

HOME ON A HILL

No. 91026

■ This plan features:

— Two bedrooms

— Two full baths

■ Sweeping panels of glass and a wood stove, creating atmosphere for the Great Room

■ An open plan that draws the Kitchen into the warmth of the Great Room's wood stove

■ A sleeping loft that has a full bath all to itself

■ A basement foundation only

FIRST FLOOR — 988 SQ. FT.
SECOND FLOOR — 366 SQ. FT.
BASEMENT — 988 SQ. FT.

TOTAL LIVING AREA:
1,354 SQ. FT.

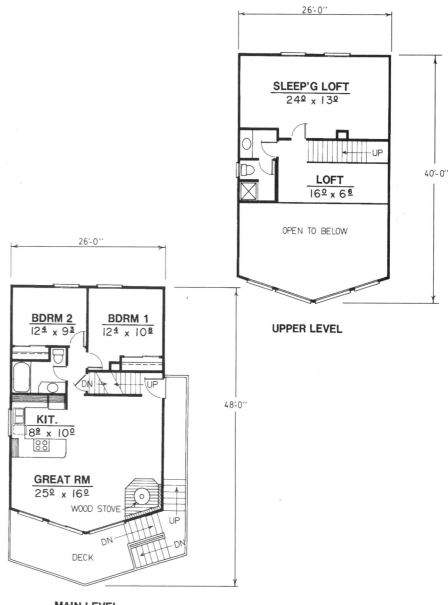

PRICE CODE A

PERFECT FOR A WATERSIDE SETTING

No. 90934

■ This plan features:

— Two bedrooms

— One full bath

■ An economical design

■ A covered sun deck adding outdoor living space

■ A mudroom/laundry area inside the side door, trapping dirt before it can enter the house

■ An open layout between the Living Room with fireplace, Dining Room and Kitchen

FIRST FLOOR — 884 SQ. FT.
WIDTH — 34'-0"
DEPTH — 28'-0"

TOTAL LIVING AREA:

884 SQ. FT.

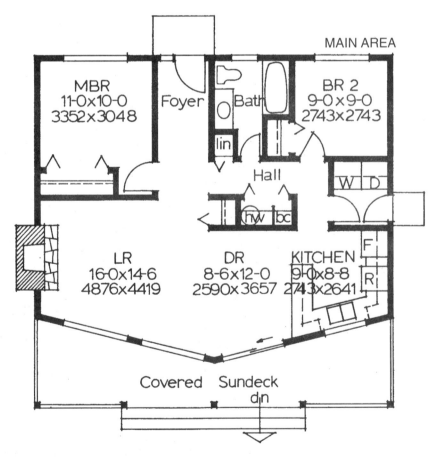

MAIN AREA

MBR
11-0x10-0
3352x3048

Foyer   Bath

BR 2
9-0 x 9-0
2743x2743

lin

Hall

W   D

LR
16-0x14-6
4876x4419

DR
8-6x12-0
2590x3657

KITCHEN
9-0x8-8
2743x2641

F

R

Covered   Sundeck
dn

An
EXCLUSIVE DESIGN
By Westhome Planners, Ltd.

PRICE CODE A

COMPACT RANCH LOADED WITH LIVING SPACE

No. 34328

■ This plan features:

— Three bedrooms

— One full bath

■ A central entrance, opening to the Living Room with ample windows

■ A Kitchen, featuring a Breakfast area with sliding doors to the backyard and an optional deck

MAIN AREA — 1,092 SQ. FT.
BASEMENT — 1,092 SQ. FT.

TOTAL LIVING AREA:
1,092 SQ. FT.

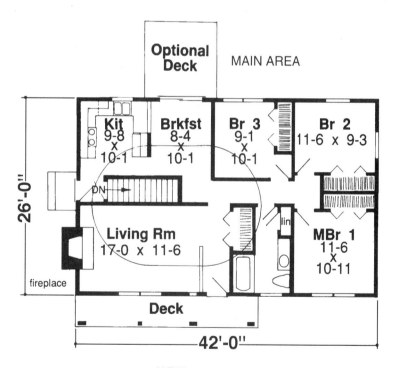

ALTERNATE FLOOR PLAN
for Crawl Space

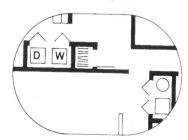

PRICE CODE A

ROOF LINES ATTRACT THE EYE

No. 26113

■ This plan features:

— Three bedrooms

— Two baths

■ Unusual roof lines which are both pleasing and balanced

■ An open floor plan shared by the Kitchen, Dining Room, Living Room and split entry spaces

■ An optional Den/Bedroom on the first floor

■ A wrap-around deck and two-car Garage adding the finishing touches to this design

FIRST FLOOR — 846 SQ. FT.
SECOND FLOOR — 492 SQ. FT.
BASEMENT — 846 SQ. FT.
GARAGE — 540 SQ. FT.
DECK — 423 SQ. FT.

TOTAL LIVING AREA:
1,338 SQ. FT.

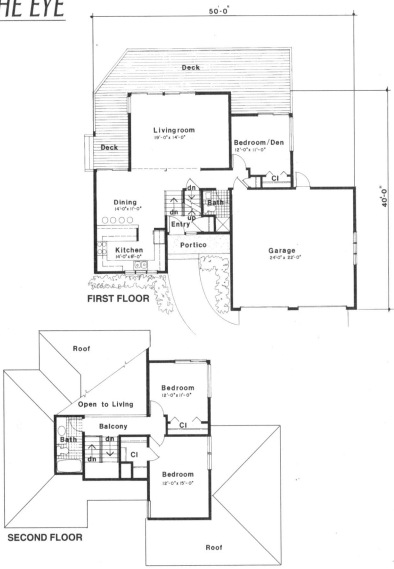

PRICE CODE A

VERSATILE CHALET

No. 90171

■ This plan features:

— Three bedrooms

— One full bath

■ A rustic, shingled exterior giving a deep woods charm

■ A large Living Room, with a stone fireplace, joining the deck through sliding doors

■ An efficient Kitchen keeping cleanup to a minimum

■ An optional basement, crawl space or pier/beam foundation — please specify when ordering

FIRST FLOOR — 780 SQ. FT.
SECOND FLOOR — 500 SQ. FT.
BASEMENT — 780 SQ. FT.

TOTAL LIVING AREA:
1,280 SQ. FT.

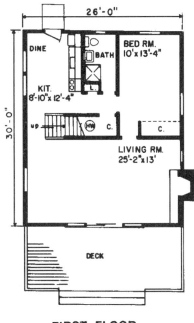

FIRST FLOOR

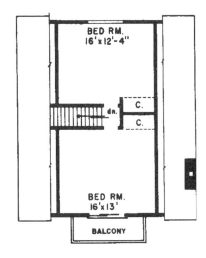

SECOND FLOOR

PRICE CODE B

WHEN THERE'S A HILL, BUILD THIS PLAN

No. 90633

■ This plan features:

— Three bedrooms

— Three full baths

■ A design for a site that slopes down

■ A sky-lit Dining Room with a high sloping ceiling and heat-circulating fireplace

■ An efficient Kitchen with a peninsula counter and all the amenities

■ A second floor Master Suite with a private balcony, deck and bath

■ A basement foundation only

FIRST FLOOR — 790 SQ. FT.
SECOND FLOOR — 453 SQ. FT.
LOWER FLOOR — 340 SQ. FT.

**TOTAL LIVING AREA:
1,583 SQ. FT.**

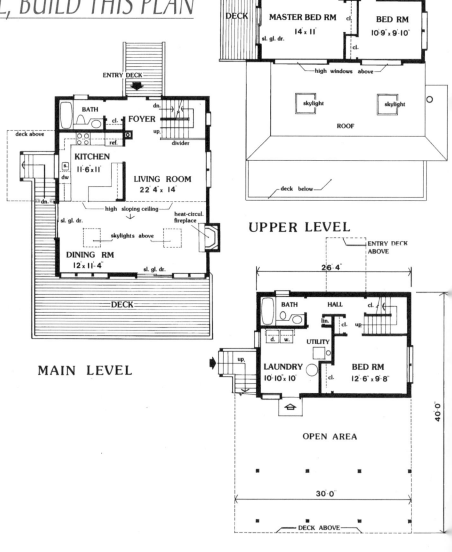

MAIN LEVEL

UPPER LEVEL

LOWER LEVEL

PRICE CODE B

HOUSE WITH MANY VIEWS

No. 90418

- This plan features:
- — Three bedrooms
- — Two full baths
- A large, open Living Room accented by a fireplace and open stairs to the second floor
- Access to the Garage through the Utility Room which adjoins Kitchen
- A large Master Bedroom with a private bath and dressing area, one wall of closets, and access to a private patio
- An optional basement, slab or crawl space foundation — please specify when ordering

FIRST FLOOR — 1,304 SQ. FT.
SECOND FLOOR — 303 SQ. FT.

**TOTAL LIVING AREA:
1,607 SQ. FT.**

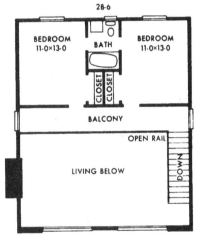

SECOND FLOOR

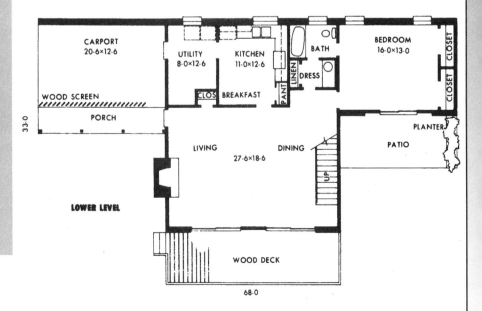

LOWER LEVEL

PRICE CODE B

A-FRAME FOR YEAR-ROUND LIVING

No. 90930

■ This plan features:

— Three bedrooms

— Two full baths

■ A vaulted ceiling in the Living Room with a massive fireplace

■ A wrap-around sun deck that gives you a lot of outdoor living space

■ A luxurious Master Suite complete with a walk-in closet, full bath and private deck

■ Two additional bedrooms that share a full hall bath

FIRST FLOOR — 1,238 SQ. FT.
LOFT — 464 SQ. FT.
BASEMENT — 1,175 SQ. FT.
WIDTH — 34'-0"
DEPTH — 56'-0"

TOTAL LIVING AREA:
1,702 SQ. FT.

An EXCLUSIVE DESIGN
By Westhome Planners, Ltd.

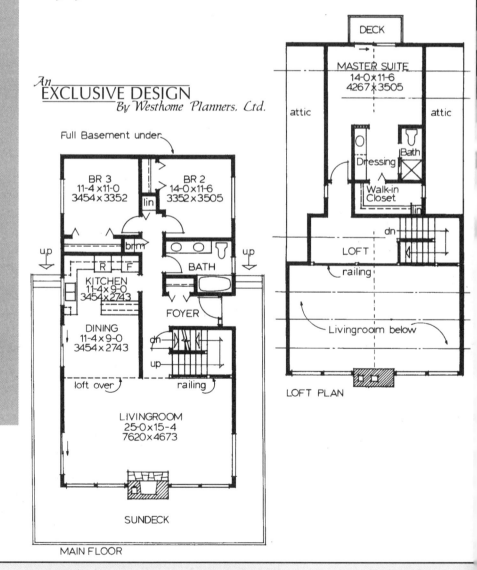

PRICE CODE B

BARN-STYLE DESIGN WITH A BALCONY

No. 91785

- This plan features:
- — Three bedrooms
- — Two full baths
- A gambrel roof and wrap-around deck to expand the living space inside and out
- A L-shaped Living/Dining Area with a tile fireplace and windows on three sides
- An efficient galley Kitchen with ample counter and storage space
- A first floor Bedroom with a private access to a full hall bath
- Two large bedrooms on the second floor, one with a private balcony, sharing a full hall bath

FIRST FLOOR — 960 SQ. FT.
SECOND FLOOR — 720 SQ. FT.
DEPTH — 40'-0"
WIDTH — 24'-0"

**TOTAL LIVING AREA;
1,680 SQ. FT.**

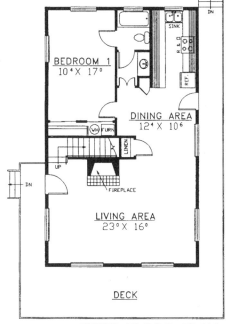

FIRST FLOOR PLAN

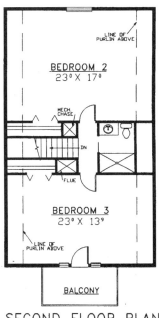

SECOND FLOOR PLAN

PRICE CODE A

COASTAL STYLE DESIGN

No. 92801

■ This plan features:

— Three bedrooms

— Two full baths

■ A wrap-around deck, sliding glass doors and many windows to enjoy the view

■ An expansive Living/Dining area

■ An efficient Kitchen with windows on two sides

■ A Master Bedroom suite with a full bath

■ A second floor Loft area with windows all around

■ A pole, slab or crawl space foundation allowing for varied building sites

FIRST FLOOR — 1,296 SQ. FT.
SECOND FLOOR — 144 SQ. FT.

TOTAL LIVING AREA:
1,440 SQ. FT.

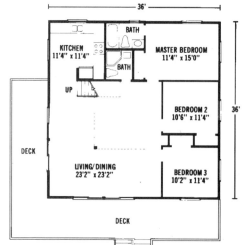

MAIN AREA

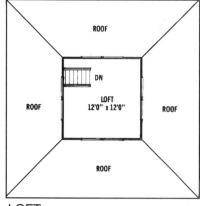

LOFT

PRICE CODE A

UNIQUE OCTAGON DESIGN

No. 91032

■ This plan features:

— Two bedrooms

— One full bath

■ A wrap-around deck for expansive views and entrance into the unusual layout through sliding glass doors

■ An open Living/Dining area with a circular fireplace and a hearth, and windows on three sides

■ An efficient, U-shaped Kitchen with ample counter space and a pass-through to the Dining area

■ A utility entrance with laundry facilities adjacent to the Kitchen

■ Two bedrooms on either side of a full hall bath with a window tub

■ Landing staircase leads to the Loft area with lots of natural light

MAIN FLOOR —1,198 SQ. FT.
LOFT —168 SQ. FT.
WIDTH — 38'-0"
DEPTH — 38'-0"

TOTAL LIVING AREA:
1,198 SQ. FT.

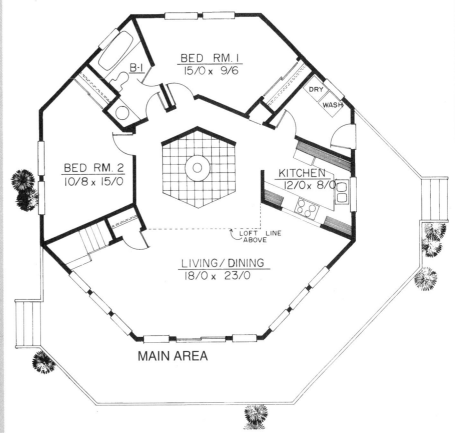

No materials list available

PRICE CODE C

UNUSUAL GLASS FRONT

No. 90167

■ This plan features:

— Four bedrooms

— Two full baths

■ A wrap-around Deck and a Dining Patio providing added outdoor living space

■ A two-story Living Room with a center fireplace and enormous windows providing natural light and a spectacular view

■ An L-shaped Kitchen with a Dining area and an adjoining Dining Patio

■ Two bedrooms on the first floor, with double closets sharing a full bath next to the Laundry area

■ Two bedrooms and a full bath on the second floor

FIRST FLOOR — 1,186 SQ. FT.
SECOND FLOOR — 692 SQ. FT.

**TOTAL LIVING AREA:
1,878 SQ. FT.**

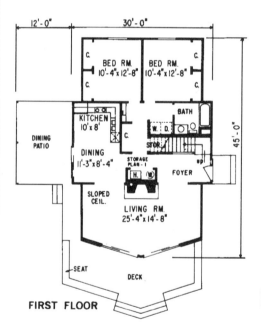

FIRST FLOOR

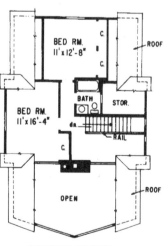

SECOND FLOOR

PRICE CODE A

Modified A-Frame at Home Anywhere

No. 90309

■ This plan features:

— One or two bedrooms

— One full and one half bath

■ A combined Living Room/Dining Room with a ceiling that reaches to the second floor loft

■ A galley-styled Kitchen conveniently arranged and open to the Dining Room

■ A fireplace in the Living Room area with sliding glass doors to the Deck

■ A loft with a half bath and an optional bedroom

First floor — 735 sq. ft.
Second floor — 304 sq. ft.

**Total living area:
1,039 sq. ft.**

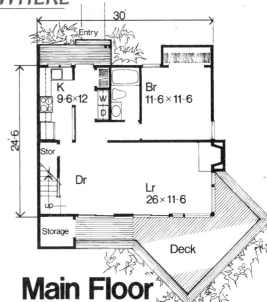

Main Floor

Second Floor

PRICE CODE A

DESIGN FEATURES SIX SIDES

No. 1074

■ This plan features:

— Three bedrooms

— Two full baths

■ Active living areas centrally located between two quiet bedroom and bath areas

■ A Living Room that can be closed off from bedroom wings giving privacy to both areas

■ A bath located behind a third bedroom

■ A bedroom complete with washer/dryer facilities.

FIRST FLOOR — 1,040 SQ. FT.
STORAGE — 44 SQ. FT.
DECK — 258 SQ. FT.
CARPORT — 230 SQ. FT.

TOTAL LIVING AREA:
1,040 SQ. FT.

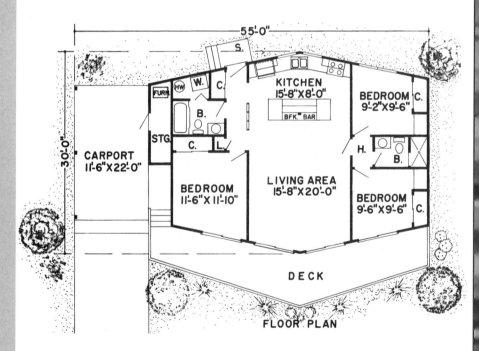

FLOOR PLAN

REAR ELEVATION

PRICE CODE D

FRONT TO BACK GLASS

No. 9840

■ This plan features:

— Two bedrooms

— Two full baths

■ A wrap-around Deck entrance leading into the two-story Living/Dining Room through double sliding glass doors

■ An efficient, U-shaped Kitchen with a counter/breakfast bar

■ A Family Room, on the lower level, with a fireplace and sliding glass doors to the covered Patio

■ Two bedrooms, with sliding doors to the rear Porch, sharing a full hall bath

■ A Sleeping Loft with a wall of windows opposite a closet and a balcony

■ An over-sized Garage leading into the Utility/Hobby Room

FIRST FLOOR — 1,120 SQ. FT.
SECOND FLOOR — 1,120 SQ. FT.
UPPER LEVEL — 340 SQ. FT.

TOTAL LIVING AREA:
2,580 SQ. FT.

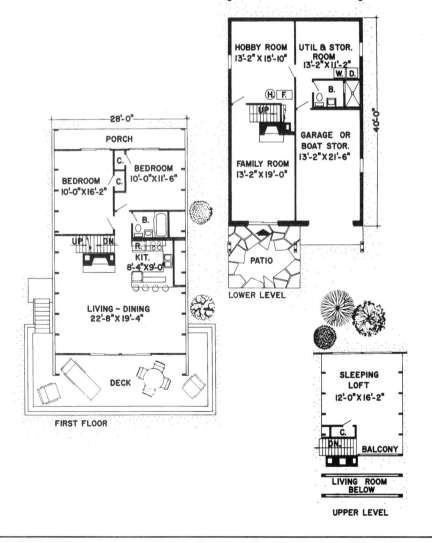

FIRST FLOOR

LOWER LEVEL

UPPER LEVEL

PRICE CODE A

AN ALPINE RETREAT

No. 98709

■ This plan features:

— Three bedrooms

— One full and one half bath

■ A wrap-around Deck providing views and access to the Living Room and the Dining area

■ An expansive Living Room with windows on three sides, a hearth fireplace and a Dining Area

■ An efficient Kitchen with ample counter and storage space serving the Dining area

■ A first level Bedroom with a double closet and private access to the full bath

■ Two additional bedrooms, one with a private Deck, sharing a half bath

FIRST FLOOR — 960 SQ. FT.
SECOND FLOOR — 420 SQ. FT.

**TOTAL LIVING AREA:
1,380 SQ. FT.**

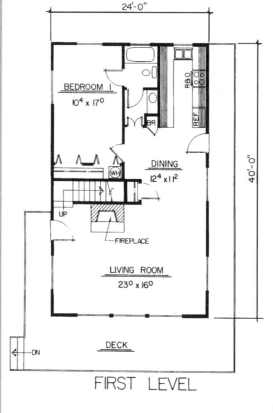

FIRST LEVEL

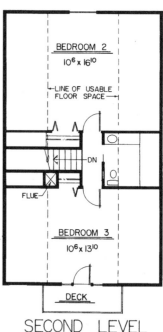

SECOND LEVEL

PRICE CODE C

SECLUDED VACATION RETREAT

No. 91704

■ This plan features:

— Two bedrooms

— Two full baths

■ A high vaulted ceiling in the Living Area with a large masonry fireplace and circular stairway

■ A wall of windows along the full cathedral height of the Living Area

■ A Kitchen with ample storage and counter space including a sink and a chopping block island

■ Private full baths for each of the bedrooms with 10 foot closets

■ A Loft with windowed doors opening to a deck

FIRST FLOOR — 1,448 SQ. FT.
LOFT — 389 SQ. FT.
CARPORT — 312 SQ. FT.

TOTAL LIVING AREA:
1,837 SQ. FT.

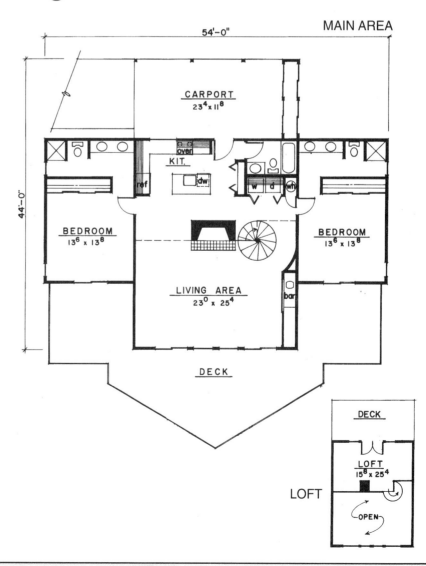

PRICE CODE A

HIGH WINDOWS ADD LIGHT

No. 26114

■ This plan features:

— Three bedrooms

— One full and one half baths

■ A covered Entry steps down into the spacious Living/Dining Room featuring a vaulted ceiling, a fireplace and sliding glass doors to expansive Deck area

■ An efficient, U-shaped Kitchen with a peninsula counter adjoining the Dining Room

■ A first floor Bedroom/Den with a triple window and a walk-in closet

■ Two additional bedrooms on the second floor share a balcony and a full bath

FIRST FLOOR — 696 SQ. FT.
SECOND FLOOR — 416 SQ. FT.
BASEMENT — 696 SQ. FT.

TOTAL LIVING AREA: 1,112 SQ. FT.

FIRST FLOOR

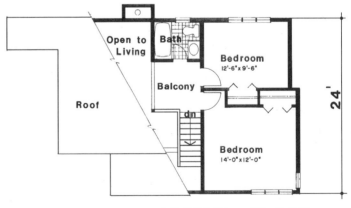

SECOND FLOOR

REAR ELEVATION

PRICE CODE E

MASTER SUITE ON A PRIVATE LEVEL

No. 26810

■ This plan features:

— Three bedrooms

— Two full baths

■ A Dining Room and sunken Living Room on a space-expanding diagonal

■ A corridor Kitchen extending into a traffic-free space open to the living areas

■ A deck, making the outdoors a natural part of all social areas

■ A Master Bedroom connecting to a Study and deck

■ A recreation area in the Lower Level

FIRST FLOOR — 1,423 SQ. FT.
LOWER FLOOR — 1,420 SQ. FT.
GARAGE — 478 SQ. FT.

TOTAL LIVING AREA: 2,843 SQ. FT.

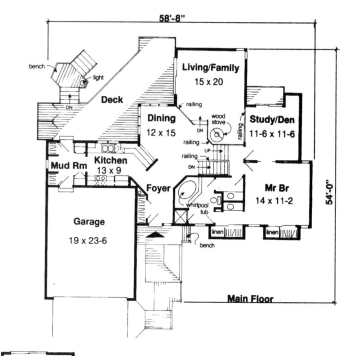

58'-8"

54'-0"

bench

light

Deck

DN

Living/Family
15 x 20

railing

Dining
12 x 15

DN

wood stove

railing

Study/Den
11-6 x 11-6

railing

Mud Rm

Kitchen
13 x 9

UP

railing

DN

Foyer

whirlpool tub

Mr Br
14 x 11-2

linen

linen

Garage
19 x 23-6

bench

Main Floor

Recreation
22 x 26

Br 2
11-6 x 11-6

UP

storage

UP

furn.

Ldry

Br 3
14 x 11

w.h.

Lower Floor

PRICE CODE A

CHALET HIDE-AWAY

No. 99707

■ This plan features:

— One bedroom

— Two full baths

■ A wrap-around Deck providing expanded living space outdoors and access into the Kitchen/Dining area

■ An open Living Area with windows on three sides, a fireplace with an over-sized hearth and a Dining area

■ An efficient, U-shaped Kitchen with ample counter space, convenient to the Dining area and the Laundry

■ A first floor Bedroom with an over-sized closet, a private entrance, and adjacent to a shower bath

■ A second floor Recreation Area with multiple uses, featuring a balcony at either end and a full bath

FIRST FLOOR — 864 SQ. FT.
SECOND FLOOR — 612 SQ. FT.

**TOTAL LIVING AREA:
1,476 SQ. FT.**

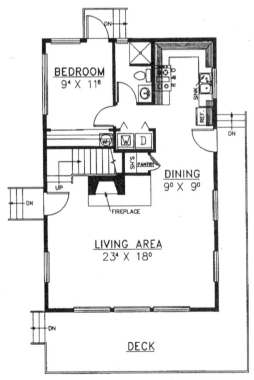

FIRST FLOOR PLAN **WIDTH 24'-0"
DEPTH 36'-0"**

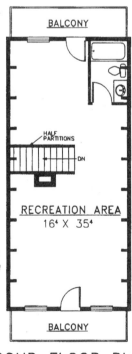

SECOND FLOOR PLAN

PRICE CODE A

*L*ET THE LIGHT SHINE IN

No. 99719

■ This plan features:

— Three bedrooms

— Two full baths

■ A main entry Deck, providing expanded living space

■ A Solarium/Living area with windows and skylights surrounding a wood stove

■ An efficient Kitchen with a built-in pantry, a garden window and a double sink island counter, convenient to the Dining area

■ A first floor Bedroom with another skylight and ample closet space

■ A Master Suite, with private access to a full bath, and an additional bedroom on the second floor

FIRST FLOOR — 414 SQ. FT.
SECOND FLOOR — 852 SQ. FT.
WIDTH — 66'-0"
DEPTH — 26'-0"

TOTAL LIVING AREA:
1,266 SQ. FT.

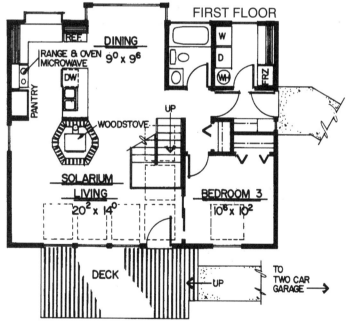

FIRST FLOOR

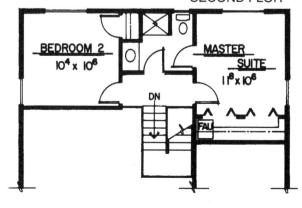

SECOND FLOR

PRICE CODE A

EASY MAINTENANCE

No. 94307

■ This plan features:

— Two bedroom

— Two full baths

■ Abundant glass and a wrap-around Deck to enjoy the out-doors

■ A tiled entrance into a large Great Room with a fieldstone fireplace and dining area below a sloped ceiling

■ A compact tiled Kitchen open to a Great Room and adjacent to the Utility area

■ Two bedrooms, one with a private bath, offer ample closet space

FIRST FLOOR — 786 SQ. FT.

TOTAL LIVING AREA: 786 SQ. FT.

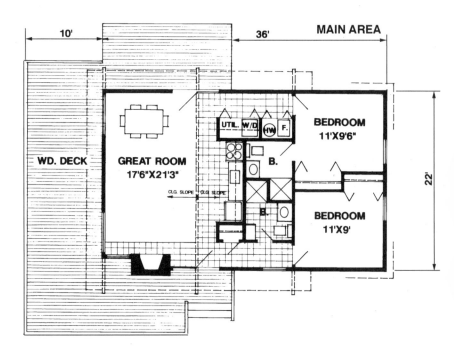

An
EXCLUSIVE DESIGN
By Marshall Associates

PRICE CODE E

COMFORTABLE OUTDOOR AND INDOOR LIVING

No. 91319

■ This plan features:

— Three bedrooms

— Three full baths

■ A wall of windows taking full advantage of the front view

■ An open stairway to the upstairs study and the Master Bedroom

■ A master bedroom with a private master bath and a walk-in wardrobe

■ An efficient Kitchen including a breakfast bar that opens into the Dining Area

■ A formal Living Room with a vaulted ceiling and a stone fireplace

FIRST FLOOR — 1,306 SQ. FT.
SECOND FLOOR — 598 SQ. FT.
LOWER FLOOR (NOT SHOWN) — 1,288 SQ. FT.

TOTAL LIVING AREA: 3,192 SQ. FT.

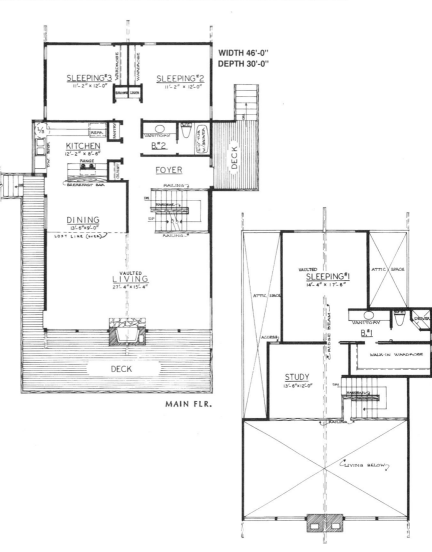

WIDTH 46'-0"
DEPTH 30'-0"

MAIN FLR.

UPPER FLR.

PRICE CODE B

FAMILY GET-AWAY

No. 34602

■ This plan features:

— Three bedrooms

— Two full baths

■ A wrap-around porch for views and visiting provides access into the Great Room and Dining area

■ A spacious Great Room with a two-story ceiling and dormer window above a massive fireplace

■ A combination Dining/Kitchen with an island work area and breakfast bar opening to the Great Room and adjacent to the laundry/storage and half-bath area

■ A private two-story Master Bedroom with dormer window, walk-in closet, double vanity bath and optional deck with hot tub

■ Two additional bedrooms on the second floor share a full hall bath

FIRST FLOOR — 1,061 SQ. FT.
SECOND FLOOR — 499 SQ. FT.
BASEMENT — 1,061 SQ. FT.

TOTAL LIVING AREA: 1,560 SQ. FT.

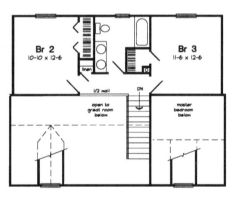

Second Floor Plan

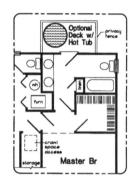

Alternate Foundation Plan

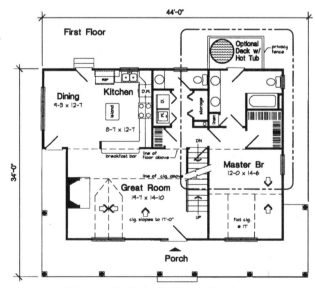

No materials list available

PRICE CODE C

No. 24704

■ This plan features:

— Three bedrooms

— Two full baths

■ A covered entry into the Great Room with a vaulted ceiling above a central fireplace/entertainment center and a wall of windows leading to an expansive Deck via an atrium door

■ An efficient, L-shaped Kitchen, with a peninsula counter, serving an open Dining Room

■ A Master Bedroom with a walk-in closet, private shower and vanity area and private

■ Two additional bedrooms on the second floor, with over-sized closets, sharing a full bath

■ A lower level Recreation area with an atrium door to a covered Patio and adjacent to a laundry area and unfinished Basement that offers many options

FIRST FLOOR — 913 SQ. FT.
SECOND FLOOR — 516 SQ. FT.
LOWER FLOOR (FINISHED) — 426 SQ. FT.

TOTAL LIVING AREA:
1,855 SQ. FT.

SPACIOUS LIVING INSIDE AND OUT

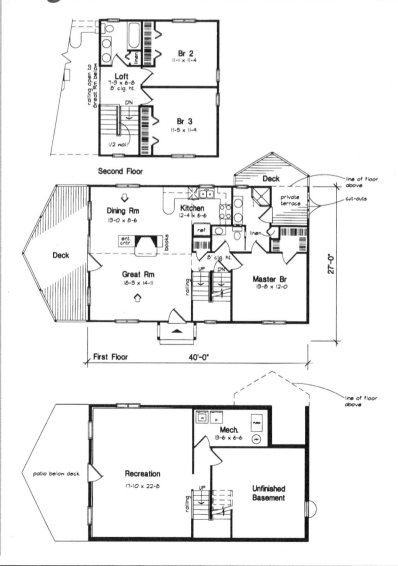

PRICE CODE E

TWO-STORY ATRIUM

No. 26870

■ This plan features:

— Three bedrooms

— Two full and one half baths

■ A two-story Atrium entrance leading into an open layout of the Living, Family and Kitchen areas

■ A spacious Living Room with a quiet Dining Room nearby

■ A Family Room with a cozy fireplace and direct access to the Deck and Kitchen

■ An airy Kitchen with a unique Solar Plant Bay

■ A private Master Suite wing with a double vanity bath

■ Two additional bedrooms on the upper level sharing a Balcony Study and full bath

■ Loads of Recreation space and Storage on the lower level

FIRST FLOOR — 1,641 SQ. FT.
SECOND FLOOR — 976 SQ. FT.
LOWER FLOOR — 1,632 SQ. FT.

**TOTAL LIVING AREA:
2,617 SQ. FT.**

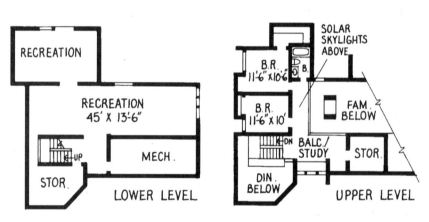

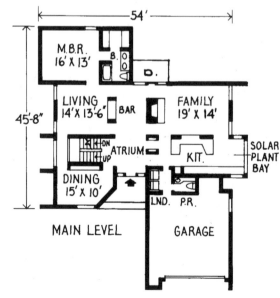

PRICE CODE C

NATURAL LIGHT AND VIEWS

No. 26760

■ This plan features:

— Three bedrooms

— Two full and one half baths

■ A sheltered entrance enhanced by skylight

■ An adjoining Living and Dining Room for easy entertaining

■ A prow-shaped Family Room highlighted by a beamed ceiling, cozy fireplace and sliding glass door to the multi-level Deck

■ An open Kitchen with a cook-top island and Breakfast area with access to a Deck

■ A Master Bedroom with a private Deck and bath with a dressing area walk-in closet

■ Two additional bedrooms near the full bath

MAIN FLOOR — 2,023 SQ. FT.
DECKS — 589 SQ. FT.

**TOTAL LIVING AREA:
2,023 SQ. FT.**

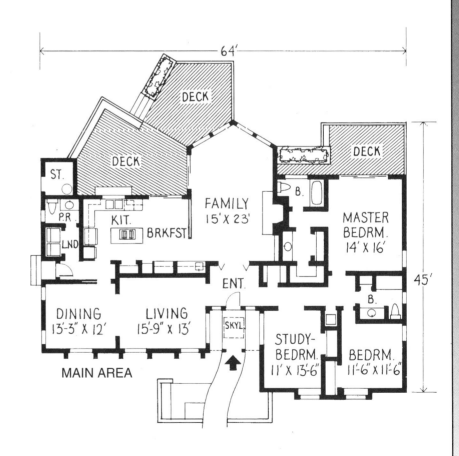

PRICE CODE A

DECK ENLARGES AND ENHANCES COTTAGE

No. 10306

■ This plan features:

— One bedroom

— One full bath

■ A large wood deck for dining, sunbathing or relaxing with friends

■ A one wall Kitchen open to the Living Room, creating simplicity and warmth.

■ A look that is ideal for both beach and mountain enthusiasts

FIRST FLOOR — 408 SQ. FT.

TOTAL LIVING AREA:
408 SQ. FT.

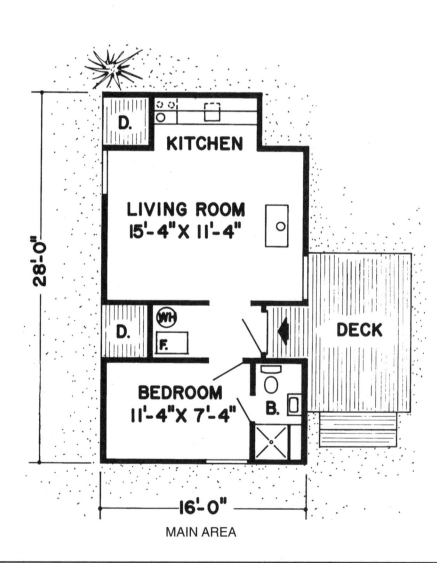

MAIN AREA

PRICE CODE A

BE IN TUNE WITH THE ELEMENTS

No. 24240

- This plan features:
— Two bedrooms
— Two full baths
- Cozy front porch to enjoy three seasons
- A simple design allowing breezes to flow from front to back, heat to rise to the attic and cool air to settle
- A fireplaced Living Room
- A formal Dining Room next to the Kitchen
- A compact Kitchen with a handy pantry
- A rear entrance with a covered porch
- A Master Suite with a private bath

MAIN AREA — 964 SQ. FT.

TOTAL LIVING AREA:
964 SQ. FT.

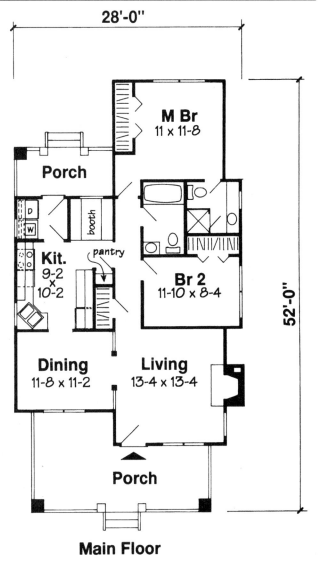

28'-0"

52'-0"

M Br
11 x 11-8

Porch

booth

Kit.
9-2 x 10-2

pantry

Br 2
11-10 x 8-4

Dining
11-8 x 11-2

Living
13-4 x 13-4

Porch

Main Floor

PRICE CODE A

CABIN WITH A GAMBREL ROOF AND EXPANSIVE DECK

No. 99701

- This plan features:
— Three bedrooms
— Two full baths
- An open-beam ceiling and six huge windows in the Living Room/Dining Room that includes a vaulted ceiling
- A private Master Suite with a full bath and two closets
- A compact Kitchen with plenty of cupboard and counter space
- Two additional small bedrooms that have the use of a full hall bath
- An average sized Utility Room with a laundry center

FIRST FLOOR — 864 SQ. FT.
SECOND FLOOR — 396 SQ. FT.
WIDTH —24'-0"
DEPTH —36'-0"

TOTAL LIVING AREA:
1,260 SQ. FT.

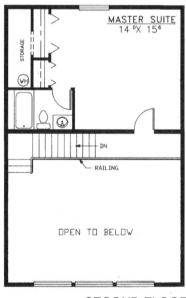

SECOND FLOOR

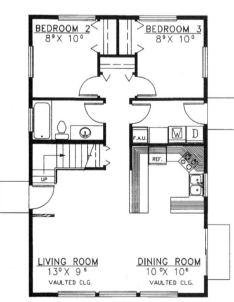

FIRST FLOOR

PRICE CODE C

FLEXIBLE FLOOR PLAN

No. 99705

■ This plan features:

— Two bedrooms plus loft

— Three full baths

■ An efficient Kitchen with an island sink/eating bar, a built-in pantry and a broom closet, which opens into the Living Room area

■ A expansive, two-story Living Room with a hearth fireplace and a wall of windows, providing access to a triangular Deck

■ Two first floor bedrooms with over-sized closets, sliding glass doors to a Deck, and private baths

■ A roomy Work Shop and a Garage providing multiple uses and ample storage space

■ A Loft area with a full bath and a sliding glass door to a private Deck

FIRST FLOOR — 1,625 SQ. FT.
SECOND FLOOR — 466 SQ. FT.
GARAGE — 742 SQ. FT.
WIDTH — 58'-0"
DEPTH — 50'-0"

TOTAL LIVING AREA: 2,091 SQ. FT.

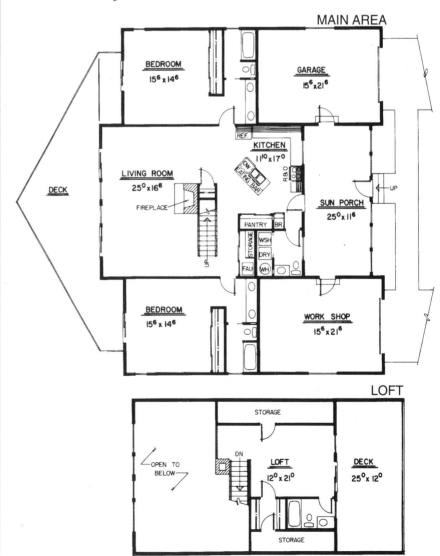

PRICE CODE A

LEISURE TIME GET-AWAY

An EXCLUSIVE DESIGN
By Marshall Associates

No. 24308

■ This plan features:

— One bedroom

— One full bath

■ The simplicity of an A-frame with a spacious feeling achieved by the large, two-story Living Room

■ An entrance deck leads into the open Living Room accented by a spiral staircase to the Loft

■ A small, but efficient Kitchen serves the Living area easily, and provides access to the full bath with a shower and a storage area

■ A first floor bedroom and a Loft area provide the sleeping quarters

FIRST FLOOR — 660 SQ. FT.
LOFT — 163 SQ. FT.

TOTAL LIVING AREA:

823 SQ. FT.

Loft
12-1 x 12-9

railing

open to below

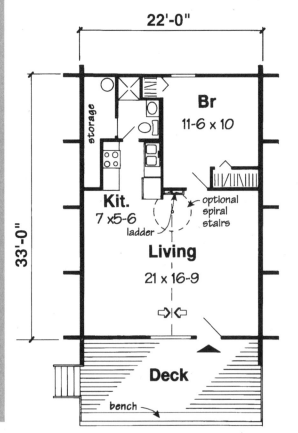

22'-0"

storage

Br
11-6 x 10

Kit.
7 x5-6

ladder

optional spiral stairs

Living
21 x 16-9

33'-0"

Deck

bench

Main Floor

PRICE CODE A

COZY RUSTIC EXTERIOR

No. 24313

■ This plan features:

— Two bedrooms

— Two full baths

■ An front deck with a double glass door entrance and large windows to either side

■ An open layout creates space and efficiency between the Kitchen and the Living Room which boasts a fireplace

■ A first floor bedroom with a double closet and a full bath

■ A second floor bedroom with double closets and a Loft area share a full bath

FIRST FLOOR — 781 SQ. FT.
SECOND FLOOR — 429 SQ. FT.

TOTAL LIVING AREA:
1,210 SQ. FT.

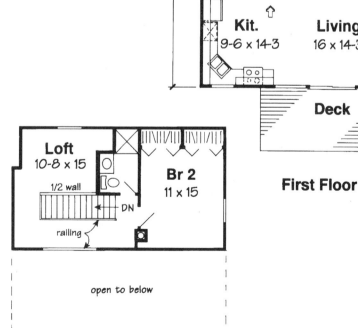

First Floor
28'-0"
30'-0"
storage
furn.
w.h.
Br 1 11 x 12-6
UP
linen
Foyer
W/D
line of floor above
Kit. 9-6 x 14-3
Living 16 x 14-3
Deck

Second Floor
Loft 10-8 x 15
1/2 wall
Br 2 11 x 15
DN
railing
open to below

An
EXCLUSIVE DESIGN
By Marshall Associates

PRICE CODE A

CONTEMPORARY ENERGY-SAVER

No. 90669

■ This plan features:

— Three bedrooms

— Three full baths plus shower

■ An enormous Deck, expanding living outdoors

■ A spacious Living Room with a sloped ceiling and a wood stove flanked by windows with built-in seats

■ An efficient, eat-in Kitchen with ample work space and easy access to all living areas

■ A first floor Bedroom with a double closet and a private Deck adjoins a full hall bath

■ Two additional bedrooms with double closets sharing a full hall bath

FIRST FLOOR — 877 SQ. FT.
SECOND FLOOR — 455 SQ. FT.

TOTAL LIVING AREA:
1,332 SQ. FT.

SECOND FLOOR PLAN

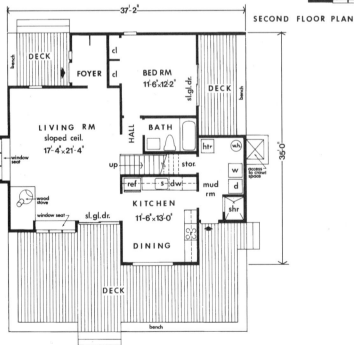

FIRST FLOOR PLAN

PRICE CODE B

SOLAR ROOM IS A UNIQUE FEATURE

No. 90611

■ This plan features:

— Three bedrooms

— Two full baths

■ A passive design that will save on heating costs

■ A heat-circulating fireplace in the Living Room adding atmosphere as well as warmth

■ A Master Suite, with lofty views of the living area

■ Two additional bedrooms with ample closet space and a shared full hall bath

■ A slab foundation only

FIRST FLOOR — 1,120 SQ. FT.
SECOND FLOOR — 490 SQ. FT.
UTILITY ROOM — 122 SQ. FT.

TOTAL LIVING AREA:
1,732 SQ. FT.

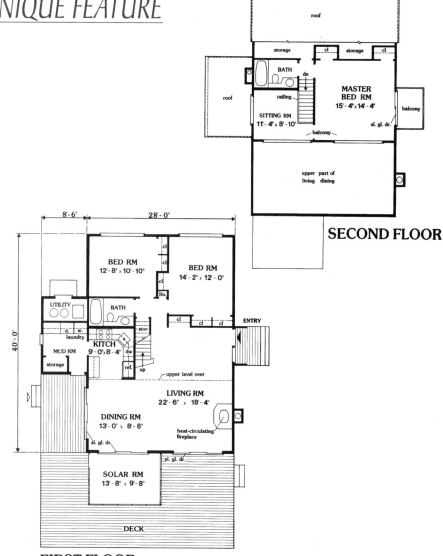

SECOND FLOOR

FIRST FLOOR

PRICE CODE A

OLD AMERICAN SALTBOX DESIGN

No. 90123

■ This plan features:

— Three bedrooms

— One and one half baths

■ A sloping Living Room ceiling that lends to spaciousness

■ A centrally located fireplace

■ Laundry facilities conveniently located off Kitchen area

■ A slab foundation only

FIRST FLOOR — 811 SQ. FT.
SECOND FLOOR — 488 SQ. FT.

TOTAL LIVING AREA: 1,299 SQ. FT.

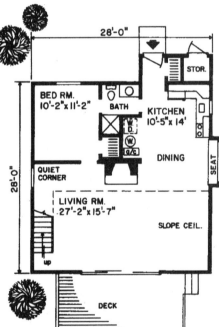

FIRST FLOOR

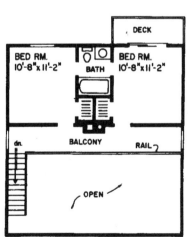

SECOND FLOOR

PRICE CODE A

THREE PORCHES OFFER OUTDOOR CHARM

No. 90048

- ■ This plan features:
- — Three bedrooms
- — Two full baths
- ■ An oversized log burning fireplace in the spacious Living/Dining area which is two stories high with sliding glass doors
- ■ Three porches offering the maximum in outdoor living space
- ■ A private bedroom located on the second floor
- ■ An efficient Kitchen including an eating bar and access to the covered Dining Porch

FIRST FLOOR — 974 SQ. FT.
SECOND FLOOR — 300 SQ. FT.

TOTAL LIVING AREA:
1,274 SQ. FT.

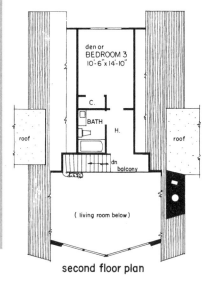

second floor plan

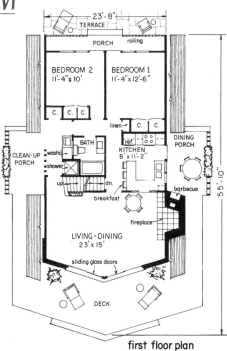

first floor plan

PRICE CODE A

YEAR ROUND RETREAT

No. 90613

■ This plan features:

— Three bedrooms

— Two full baths

■ A Living Room with a dramatic sloping ceiling and a wood burning stove

■ A Kitchen and Living Room opening onto the rear deck

■ A Master Suite with a full bath, linen closet and ample closet space

FIRST FLOOR — 967 SQ. FT.
SECOND FLOOR — 465 SQ. FT.

**TOTAL LIVING AREA:
1,432 SQ. FT.**

SECOND FLOOR

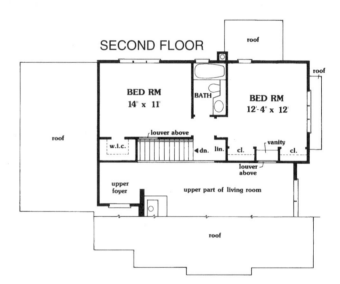

FIRST FLOOR

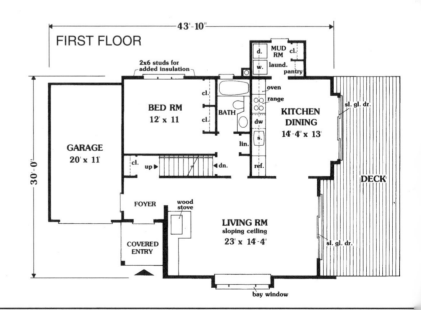

REAR ELEVATION

PRICE CODE A

BUILD THIS ONE IN STAGES

No. 90638

■ This plan features:

— Three bedrooms

— Two full baths

■ A covered entrance into spacious Living/Dining Area with a 13 foot cathedral ceiling, fireplace and two sliding glass doors to a huge Deck

■ An efficient L-shaped Kitchen with separate counter space for dining is adjacent to Deck and Laundry/Utility room

■ A Master Bedroom with a private shower bath

■ Two additional bedrooms sharing a full hall bath

■ An option to build in stages

STAGE ONE — 700 SQ. FT.
STAGE TWO — 342 SQ. FT.

TOTAL LIVING AREA:
1,042 SQ. FT.

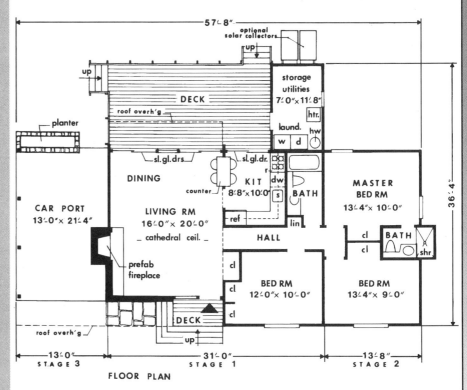

FLOOR PLAN

PRICE CODE A

SNUG RETREAT WITH A VIEW

No. 91031

■ This plan features:

— One bedroom plus loft

— One full bath

■ A large front Deck providing views and an expansive entrance

■ A two-story Living/Dining area with double glass doors leading out to the Deck

■ An efficient, U-shaped Kitchen with a pass through counter to the Dining area

■ A first floor Bedroom, with ample closet space, located near a full shower bath

■ A Loft/Bedroom on the second floor offering multiple uses

MAIN FLOOR — 572 SQ. FT.
LOFT — 308 SQ. FT.

TOTAL LIVING AREA:
880 SQ. FT.

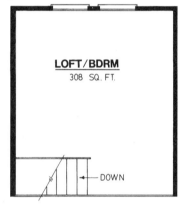

LOFT/BDRM
308 SQ. FT.

DOWN

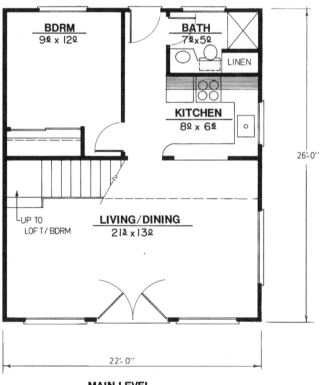

BDRM
9⁰ x 12⁰

BATH
7⁰ x 5⁰

LINEN

KITCHEN
8⁰ x 6⁸

26'-0"

UP TO
LOFT / BDRM

LIVING/DINING
21⁸ x 13⁰

22'-0"

MAIN LEVEL

PRICE CODE A

SUITED FOR A HILL

No. 90822

■ This plan features:

— Three bedrooms

— One and a half baths

■ Vaulted ceilings and a fieldstone fireplace in the Living/Dining Room

■ Two first floor bedrooms that have ample closet space and share a full hall bath

■ A Master Bedroom on the loft level including a private bath

■ A wrap-around sun deck offering an abundance of outdoor living space

FIRST FLOOR — 925 SQ. FT.
LOFT — 338 SQ. FT.
BASEMENT — 864 SQ. FT.
WIDTH — 33'-0"
DEPTH — 47'-0"

TOTAL LIVING AREA:
1,263 SQ. FT.

An
EXCLUSIVE DESIGN
By Westhome Planners, Ltd.

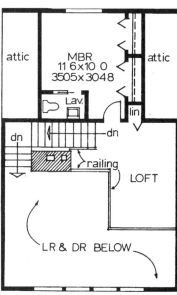

LOFT PLAN

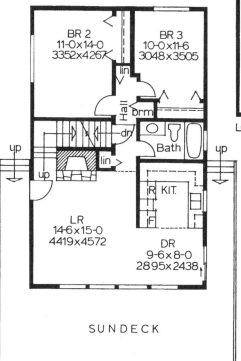

MAIN FLOOR

PRICE CODE D

No. 10542

■ This plan features:

— Four bedrooms

— Three full baths

■ A tile Entry leading into a two-story Living Room with a corner fireplace and two levels of windows above the Window Seat

■ A central Kitchen with a peninsula counter, double sink, built-in desk

■ A Master Bedroom suite with a walk-in closet and a bath with a Jacuzzi

■ On the upper level, another Bedroom with a private bath, a Study and a Loft overlooking Living Room

■ Two additional bedrooms, with walk-in closets, share a full bath on the lower level

MAIN FLOOR — 1,106 SQ. FT.
LOWER LEVEL (FINISHED) — 746 SQ. FT.
UPPER FLOOR — 722 SQ. FT.
GARAGE — 645 SQ. FT.

TOTAL LIVING AREA: 2,574 SQ. FT.

OPEN LOFT ADDS CHARM

An EXCLUSIVE DESIGN *By Karl Kreeger*

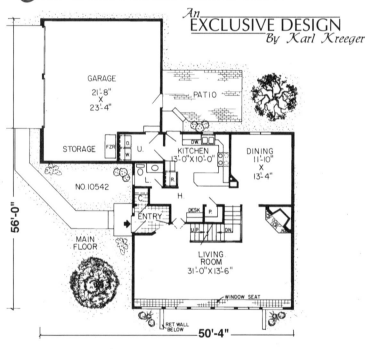

PRICE CODE A

ONE FLOOR LIVING WITH EXPANSIVE STORAGE

No. 10234

■ This plan features:

— Two bedrooms

— One and a half baths

■ A huge Living Room with double sliding glass doors leading to a large Balcony

■ A country Kitchen with a built-in pantry, dining space and optional sliding glass doors to the deck

■ Two over-sized bedrooms, one adjacent to a Laundry area, with double closets and sharing a full hall bath

■ A lower level with two Garages, one large enough for a camper, offers a built-in workbench and plenty of storage space

UPPER LEVEL — 1,254 SQ. FT.
LOWER LEVEL — 1,064 SQ. FT.

TOTAL LIVING AREA:
1,254 SQ. FT.

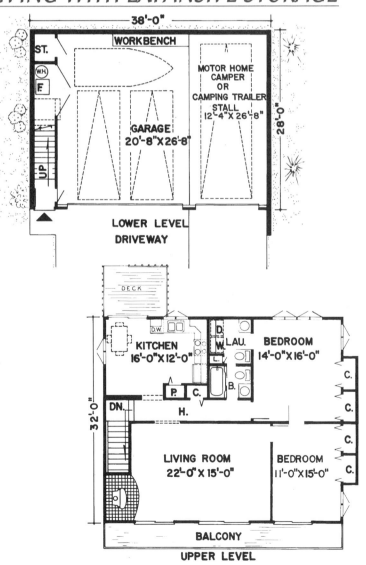

PRICE CODE C

NATURAL LIGHT ALL AROUND

No. 92806

■ This plan features:

— Three bedrooms

— Two full baths

■ A Foyer leading into the Great Room with a huge fieldstone fireplace, a cathedral ceiling and highlighted by an angled wall of windows with two sets of sliding glass doors to an optional deck

■ An L-shaped Kitchen/Dining area, adjacent to the laundry area, with angled windows and a sliding glass door

■ A Master Bedroom suite with a private bath, two closets and large angled windows

■ Two additional bedrooms on the second floor sharing a full hall bath

■ A basement, slab or crawl space foundation available — please specify when ordering

FIRST FLOOR — 1,323 SQ. FT.
SECOND FLOOR — 518 SQ. FT.

TOTAL LIVING AREA:
1,841 SQ. FT.

FIRST FLOOR

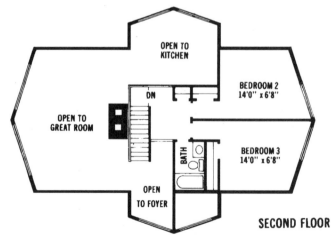

SECOND FLOOR

PRICE CODE B

VACATION IN STYLE

No. 92803

■ This plan features:

— Four bedrooms

— Two full baths

■ A long wooden Deck and a Screened Porch providing outdoor living space

■ An expansive Great Room/Dining Area with a fireplace and glass on three sides

■ An efficient Kitchen with ample storage space and an open counter separating it from the Dining area

■ A Master Bedroom with windows on two sides and a walk-in closet adjacent to a full hall bath

■ A pole, slab or crawl space foundation allowing for varied building sites

MAIN FLOOR — 1,600 SQ. FT.

TOTAL LIVING AREA:
1,600 SQ. FT.

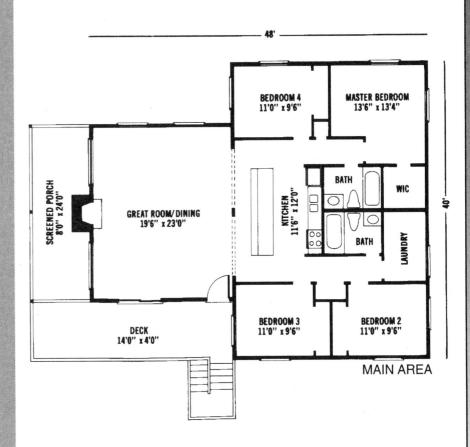

48'

40'

BEDROOM 4
11'0" x 9'6"

MASTER BEDROOM
13'6" x 13'4"

SCREENED PORCH
8'0" x 24'0"

GREAT ROOM/DINING
19'6" x 23'0"

KITCHEN
11'6" x 12'0"

BATH

WIC

BATH

LAUNDRY

DECK
14'0" x 4'0"

BEDROOM 3
11'0" x 9'6"

BEDROOM 2
11'0" x 9'6"

MAIN AREA

PRICE CODE B

GLASS CAPTURES VIEWS & SUN IN A-FRAME

No. 90121

■ This plan features:

— Three bedrooms

— Two full baths

■ Large exterior exposed beams

■ A Family Room with sliders to the deck

■ Wooden seats railing the deck which flows into a dining patio on the left side

■ A Master Bedroom including a large fireplaced sitting area

■ An optional basement, slab or crawl space foundation — please specify when ordering

FIRST FLOOR — 1,126 SQ. FT.
SECOND FLOOR — 624 SQ. FT.
BASEMENT — 1,100 SQ. FT.

**TOTAL LIVING AREA:
1,750 SQ. FT.**

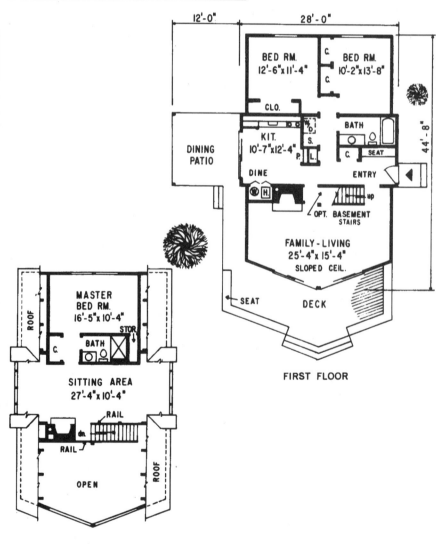

SECOND FLOOR

FIRST FLOOR

PRICE CODE A

A TUTOR-STYLE GEM

No. 90172

■ This plan features:

— One bedroom

— One full bath

■ A private, sheltered stairway

■ Secure storage in the Garage for recreational vehicles or boats

■ A deck off the Dining area for outdoor living space

■ A roomy Living Room that flows into the Dining area for a more spacious feeling

■ A good-sized bedroom

■ Laundry facilities located next to the efficient Kitchen

FIRST FLOOR — 784 SQ. FT.
GARAGE — 784 SQ. FT.

TOTAL LIVING AREA:
784 SQ. FT.

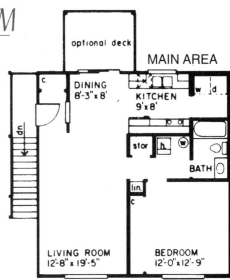

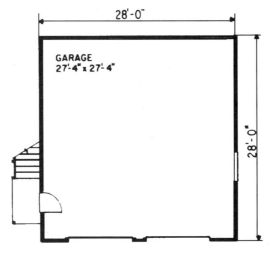

PRICE CODE A

VACATION RETREAT OR YEAR ROUND LIVING

No. 1078

■ This plan features:

— Two bedrooms

— One full bath

■ A long hallway dividing bed-rooms and living areas assuring privacy

■ A centrally located utility room and bath

■ An open Living/Dining Room area with exposed beams, sloping ceilings and optional fireplace

FIRST FLOOR — 1,024 SQ. FT.
CARPORT & STORAGE — 387 SQ. FT.
DECK — 411 SQ. FT.

TOTAL LIVING AREA:
1,024 SQ. FT.

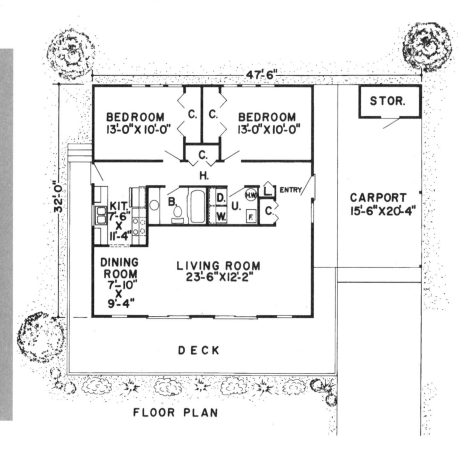

FLOOR PLAN

PRICE CODE A

RUSTIC VACATION HOUSE

No. 90004

■ This plan features:

— Three bedrooms

— One full and one half baths

■ Two porches and an outdoor balcony for entertaining, relaxing or just enjoying a sunset

■ A spiral stairway leading to the balcony and upstairs bedroom

■ A Living Room with a massive stone fireplace, floor-to-ceiling windows at the gable end, and sliding glass doors to a rear porch

■ A pantry adjoining the Kitchen which has a small bay window over the sink

FIRST FLOOR — 1,020 SQ. FT.
SECOND FLOOR — 265 SQ. FT.

TOTAL LIVING AREA:
1,285 SQ. FT.

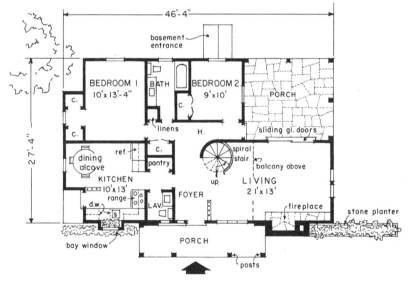

first floor

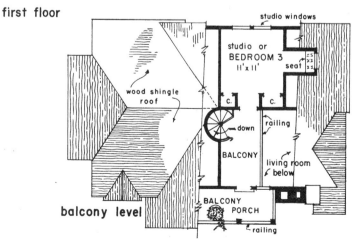

balcony level

PRICE CODE A

VERSATILE CHALET

An
EXCLUSIVE DESIGN
By Westhome Planners, Ltd.

No. 90847

■ This plan features:

— Two bedrooms

— Two full baths

■ A Sun deck entry into a spacious Living Room/Dining Room with a fieldstone fireplace, a large window and a sliding glass door

■ A well-appointed Kitchen with extended counter space and easy access to the Dining Room and the Utility area

■ A first floor bedroom adjoins a full hall bath

■ A spacious Master Bedroom, with a private Deck, a Suite bath and plenty of storage

FIRST FLOOR — 864 SQ. FT.
SECOND FLOOR — 496 SQ. FT.
WIDTH — 27'-0"
DEPTH — 32'-0"

TOTAL LIVING AREA:
1,360 SQ. FT.

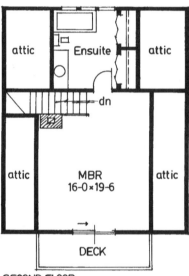

SECOND FLOOR

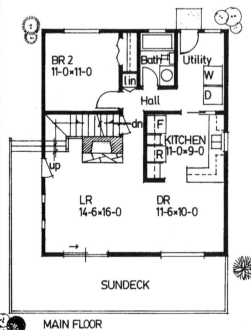

MAIN FLOOR

PRICE CODE B

ENJOY THE VIEWS

No. 90859

■ This plan features:

— Three bedrooms

— One and a half baths

■ A wrap-around Sundeck

■ A spacious Living/Dining Room with a vaulted ceiling and a wood stove flanked by a wall of glass

■ A Mudroom/Utility entrance with a laundry area and ample closets

■ An efficient, U-shaped Kitchen with a snack bar separating the Dining area

■ A first floor bedroom adjacent to a half bath

■ A second floor Master Bedroom, Loft and secondary bedroom sharing the full hall bath

FIRST FLOOR — 843 SQ. FT.
SECOND FLOOR — 768 SQ. FT.

TOTAL LIVING AREA:
1,611 SQ. FT.

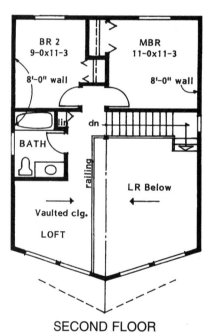

SECOND FLOOR

FIRST FLOOR

WIDTH — 28'-0"
DEPTH — 48'-6"

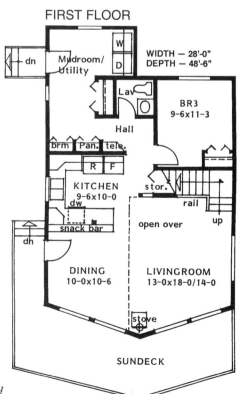

An
EXCLUSIVE DESIGN
By Westhome Planners, Ltd.

PRICE CODE A

MOUNTAIN RETREAT

No. 34625

■ This plan features:

— Two bedrooms

— Two full baths

■ A Deck entrance through double sliding glass doors into a spacious Living Room with a cozy fireplace and a sloped ceiling

■ An efficient, U-shaped Kitchen with an open counter to the Living Room and a view

■ A Master Bedroom with a double closet, full bath and a laundry

■ An upper level with a Bedroom and a Loft sharing a full bath

FIRST FLOOR — 780 SQ. FT
SECOND FLOOR — 451 SQ. FT.

**TOTAL LIVING AREA:
1,231 SQ. FT.**

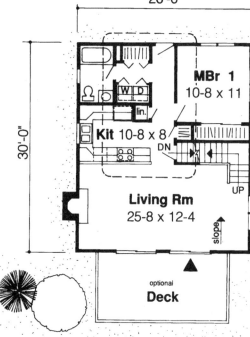

26'-0"

30'-0"

MBr 1 10-8 x 11

Kit 10-8 x 8

DN

Living Rm 25-8 x 12-4

slope

UP

optional
Deck

Main Level

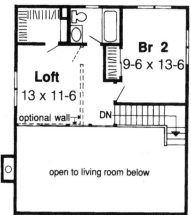

Loft 13 x 11-6

optional wall

Br 2 9-6 x 13-6

DN

open to living room below

Upper Level

W | D

lin.

Slab/Crawlspace Option

PRICE CODE A

DELIGHTFUL, COMPACT HOME

No. 34003

■ This plan features:

— Three bedrooms

— Two full baths

■ A fireplaced Living Room brightened by a wonderful picture window

■ A counter island featuring double sinks separating the Kitchen and Dining areas

■ A Master Bedroom that includes a private Master Bath and double closets

■ Two additional bedrooms with ample closet space that share a full bath

FIRST FLOOR — 1,146 SQ. FT.

**TOTAL LIVING AREA:
1,146 SQ. FT.**

44'-0"

28'-0"

Br 2
10 x 12-8

Br 3
10 x 9-4

Kit
10 x 11

Dining
9 x 11

slope slope

DN

linen

Living Rm
19 x 12-4

MBr 1
13-4 x 12

Deck

Floor Plan

W

D

slab/crawlspace option

PRICE CODE D

DECK SURROUNDS HOUSE ON THREE SIDES

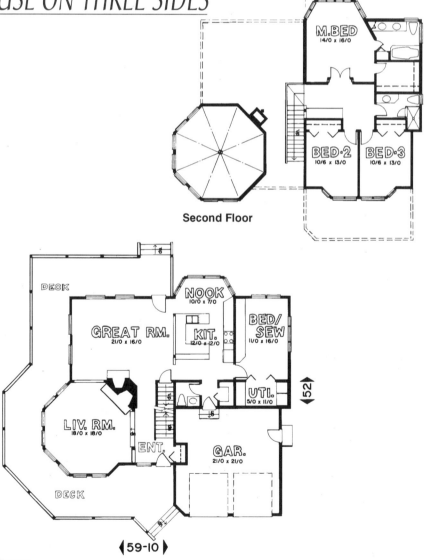

Second Floor

No. 91304

■ This plan features:

— Three bedrooms

— Two full and one half baths

■ A sunken, circular Living Room with windows on four sides and a vaulted clerestory for a wide-open feeling

■ Back-to-back fireplaces in the Living Room and the adjoining Great Room

■ A convenient, efficient Kitchen with a sunny eating Nook

■ A Master Suite with a walk-in closet and a private Master Bath

■ Two additional bedrooms that share a full hall bath

FIRST FLOOR — 1,439 SQ. FT.
SECOND FLOOR — 873 SQ. FT.

**TOTAL LIVING AREA:
2,312 SQ. FT.**

PRICE CODE B

TOWERING WINDOWS

No materials list available

No. 91071

■ This plan features:

— Three bedrooms

— Two full baths

■ A wrap-around Deck above a three car garage with plenty of work/storage space

■ Both the Dining and Living areas claim vaulted ceilings above French doors to the Deck

■ A octagon-shaped Kitchen with a view, a cooktop peninsula and an open counter to the Dining area

■ A Master Bedroom on the upper level, with an over-sized closet, a private bath and an optional Loft

■ Two additional bedrooms sharing a full hall bath

FIRST FLOOR — 1,329 SQ. FT.
SECOND FLOOR — 342 SQ. FT.
GARAGE — 885 SQ. FT.
DECK — 461 SQ. FT.

**TOTAL LIVING AREA:
1,671 SQ. FT.**

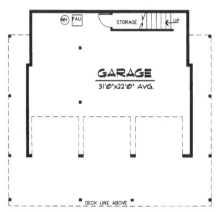

LOWER FLOOR

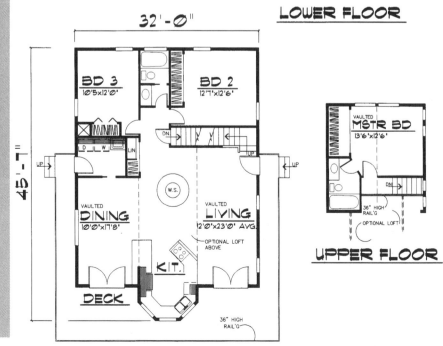

MAIN FLOOR PLAN

UPPER FLOOR

PRICE CODE B

ALL ON ONE FLOOR

No. 92805

■ This plan features:

— Three bedrooms

— Two full baths

■ A covered entrance into the Foyer that leads to the Dining/Family area and the Living Room, topped by a cathedral ceiling and separated by a massive fieldstone fireplace

■ Sliding glass doors with windows above to optional decks offering front to back natural lighting and views

■ A efficient, galley Kitchen adjacent to the Dining and the Laundry areas

■ A private Master Bedroom suite with large windows, a walk-in closet and a full bath

■ Two additional bedrooms served by a full hall bath

MAIN FLOOR — 1,768 SQ. FT.

TOTAL LIVING AREA:
1,768 SQ. FT.

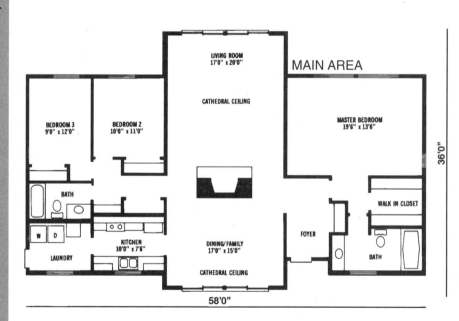

PRICE CODE B

*I*DEAL FOR COASTAL VIEW

No. 92802

■ This plan features:

— Three bedrooms

— Two full baths

■ A wrap-around Deck and windows to the summit of the cathedral ceiling in the Dining/Living areas

■ An efficient, U-shaped Kitchen with a pass-through counter to the Dining area

■ A private bath, and ample closet space in the Master Bedroom suite

■ Two additional bedrooms sharing a full hall bath

■ A Loft area expanding the living space or storage

■ A pole, slab or craw space foundation allowing for varied building sites

FIRST FLOOR — 1,320 SQ. FT.
SECOND FLOOR — 185 SQ. FT.

TOTAL LIVING AREA:
1,505 SQ. FT.

FIRST FLOOR

44'

MASTER BEDROOM 14'6" x 14'6"

BEDROOM 2 13'6" x 11'0"

BATH

BEDROOM 3 9'0" x 14'6"

DN   UP

BATH

KITCHEN 9'0" x 10'0"

CATHEDRAL CEILING

DINING-LIVING 28'6" x 14'6"

30'

DECK

SECOND FLOOR

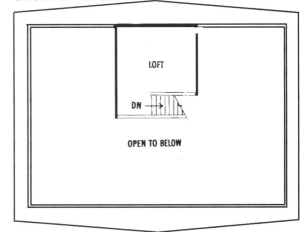

LOFT

DN

OPEN TO BELOW

PRICE CODE A

CONTEMPORARY SIMPLICITY

No. 24307

■ This plan features:

— Two bedrooms

— Two full baths

■ A tile entrance leading into a two-story, beamed Living Room with a circular, center fireplace

■ An efficient, U-shaped Kitchen, with plenty of counter and storage space opens into the Dining area with sliding glass doors to an optional Deck

■ Two bedrooms, one with a private shower, both with ample closet space

■ A second floor Loft overlooking the living area

FIRST FLOOR — 866 SQ. FT.
LOFT — 172 SQ. FT.

**TOTAL LIVING AREA:
1,038 SQ. FT.**

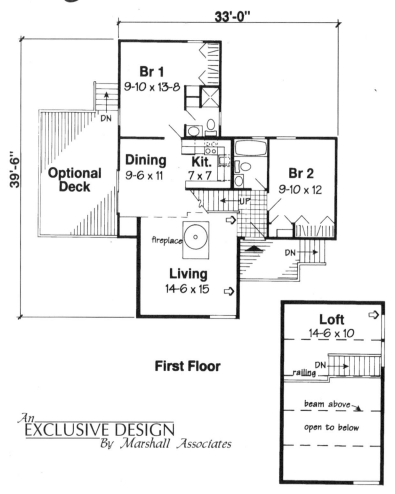

First Floor

An EXCLUSIVE DESIGN
By Marshall Associates

Loft

PRICE CODE C

COMFORTABLE VACATION LIVING

No. 98714

■ This plan features:

— Three bedrooms

— Three full and one half baths

■ A wrap-around Deck offering views and access into the Living Room

■ A sunken Living Room with a vaulted ceiling, and a raised-hearth fireplace adjoining the Dining area

■ An open Kitchen with a corner sink and windows, an eating bar and a walk-in storage/pantry

■ Two private Bedroom suites with sliding glass doors leading to a Deck, walk-in closets and plush baths

■ A Loft area with a walk-in closet, attic access, and a private bath and a Deck

FIRST FLOOR — 1,704 SQ FT
SECOND FLOOR — 313 SQ. FT.

TOTAL LIVING AREA:
2,017 SQ. FT.

FLOOR PLAN

LOFT PLAN

PRICE CODE

CLASSIC CABIN DESIGN

No. 90168

■ This plan features:

— Three bedrooms plus bunk room

— One full bath

■ An Entry into a large Family Room with a fieldstone fireplace situated between two sets of sliding glass doors

■ A large wrap-around Deck that expands the living space

■ A step-saving Kitchen with an eating bar

■ First floor Bedroom with a double closet adjoins a full hall bath

■ A bunk room to supplement the large bedrooms

■ A second floor that claims two bedrooms with ample closet and storage space

FIRST FLOOR — 884 SQ. FT.
SECOND FLOOR — 550 SQ. FT.

TOTAL LIVING AREA:
1,434 SQ. FT.

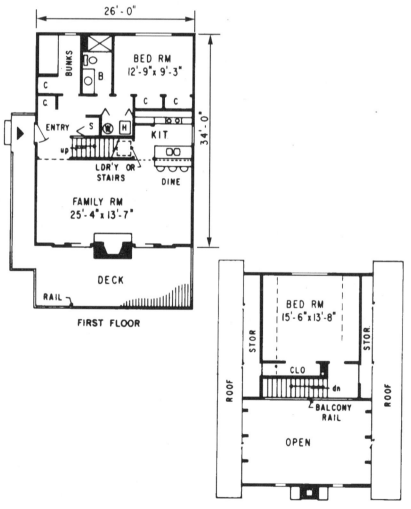

PRICE CODE A

OPEN FLOOR PLAN ENHANCES HOME

No. 90307

■ This plan features:

— One bedroom

— Two full baths

■ A Fireside Room with a vaulted ceiling and a unique built-in sofa enclosed in glass with a focal point fireplace

■ A centrally-located island Kitchen efficiently laid out and flowing into the Dining Room

■ A second floor bedroom incorporating a bump-out window and a sitting room

FIRST FLOOR — 768 SQ. FT.
SECOND FLOOR — 419 SQ. FT.

TOTAL LIVING AREA:
1,187 SQ. FT.

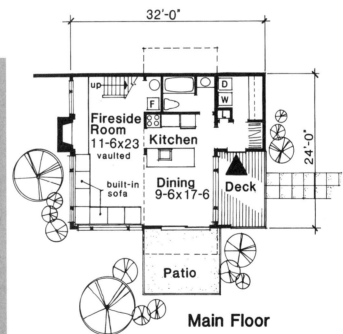

Main Floor

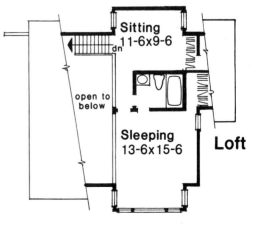

Loft

PRICE CODE A

UNUSUAL A-FRAME

No. 10228

■ This plan features:

— Two bedrooms

— One and a half baths

■ A covered Entry leading down to a large Living Room with a cheerful, metal fireplace

■ An L-shaped Kitchen opening into a Family Room with sliding glass doors to the Patio

■ An upper level with two spacious bedrooms and private Decks sharing a full hall bath

FIRST FLOOR — 768 SQ. FT.
SECOND FLOOR — 521 SQ. FT.

TOTAL LIVING AREA:
1,289 SQ. FT.

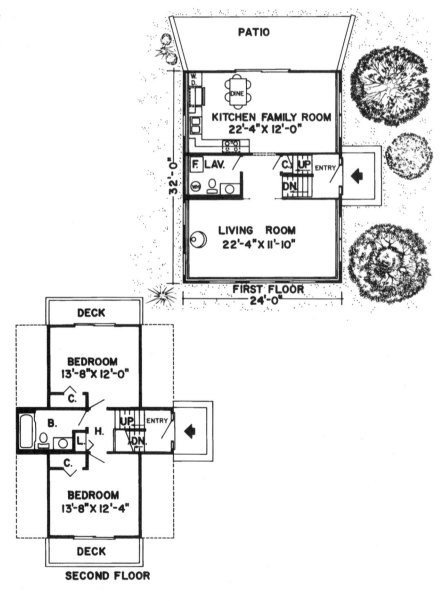

PRICE CODE A

COMPACT AND OPEN CABIN

No. 84020

■ This plan features:

— Three bedrooms

— One full bath

■ An open Living Room leading into an efficient Kitchen

■ Three bedrooms, with ample closets, sharing a full hall bath

■ A full basement option or a separate washer and dryer area

MAIN FLOOR — 768 SQ. FT.

TOTAL LIVING AREA:
768 SQ. FT.

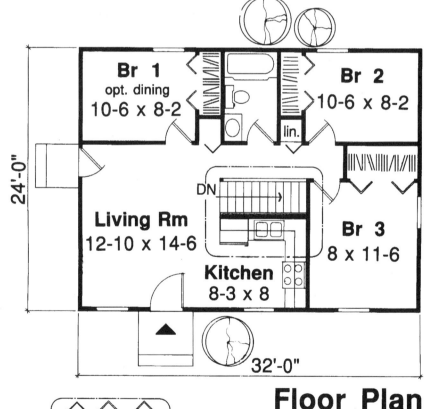

Br 1
opt. dining
10-6 x 8-2

Br 2
10-6 x 8-2

lin.

DN

Living Rm
12-10 x 14-6

Br 3
8 x 11-6

Kitchen
8-3 x 8

24'-0"

32'-0"

Floor Plan

No materials list available

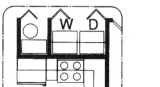

Slab/Crawlspace Option

ANGLED FOR VIEWS

No. 9107

- This plan features:
- — Four Bedrooms
- — Two full baths
- A large Foyer leading into the Living Room, the Family Room and the Kitchen
- A spacious Living Room with large windows and a sliding glass door to the Balcony, shared by the Family Room with the same features
- An efficient, U-shaped Kitchen with a laundry and eating space
- A Master Bedroom suite with an over-sized closet and a vanity bath
- Two additional bedrooms with ample closets, sharing a full hall bath

FIRST FLOOR — 2,051 SQ. FT.
BASEMENT — 1,380 SQ. FT.
GARAGE — 671 SQ. FT.

TOTAL LIVING AREA:
2,051 SQ. FT.

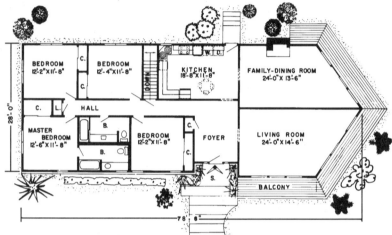

PRICE CODE C

PRICE CODE A

VACATION BLISS

No. 10012

- This plan features:
- — Three bedrooms
- — Two and one half baths
- A redwood deck that adapts equally to both lake and ocean settings
- A Family Room measuring 36 feet long and leading out to a shaded patio
- Fireplaces in both the Living Room and Family Room
- An open Kitchen with a laundry room for convenience

FIRST FLOOR — 1,198 SQ. FT.
BASEMENT — 1,198 SQ. FT.

TOTAL LIVING AREA:
1,198 SQ. FT.

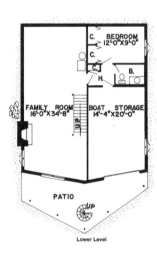

Lower Level

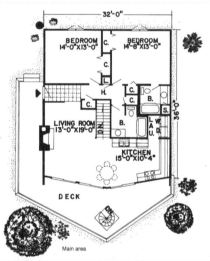

Main area

PRICE CODE B

COMPACT HOME DESIGN

No. 10455

■ This plan features:

— Three bedrooms

— Two full baths

■ An airlock Entry that saves energy

■ A Living Room with an entire wall of windows, fireplace, built-in bookcases, and a wetbar

■ A step-saver Kitchen with an abundance of storage and a convenient peninsula

■ A Master Bedroom with separate vanities and walk-in closets

MAIN AREA — 1,643 SQ. FT.
GARAGE — 500 SQ. FT.

**TOTAL LIVING AREA:
1,643 SQ. FT.**

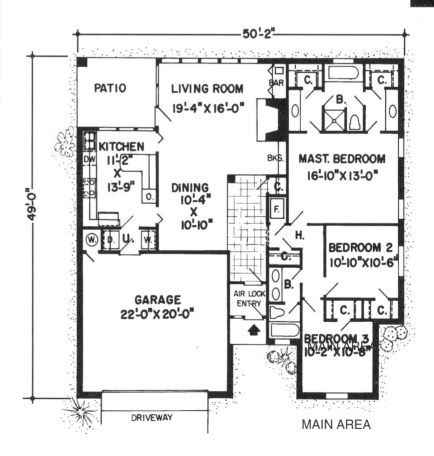

PRICE CODE B

SUNSHINE SPECIAL

No. 20150

■ This plan features:

— Three bedrooms

— Two full baths

■ A Living Room with a large fire-place and a sloped ceiling.

■ A walk-in closet in each bedroom

■ A Master Suite including a luxury bath and a decorative ceiling

FIRST FLOOR — 1,638 SQ. FT.
BASEMENT — 1,320 SQ. FT.
GARAGE — 462 SQ. FT.

TOTAL LIVING AREA:
1,638 SQ. FT.

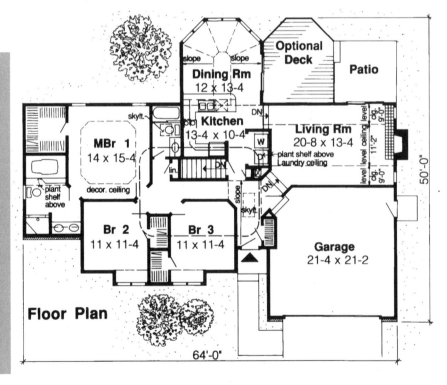

Floor Plan

An
EXCLUSIVE DESIGN
By Karl Kreeger

Slab/Crawl Space Option

PRICE CODE B

PORCH INSPIRES ROCKING CHAIR RELAXING

No. 90409

■ This plan features:

— Three bedrooms

— Two full baths

■ A massive fireplace separating Living and Dining Rooms

■ An isolated Master Suite with a walk-in closet and compartmentalized bath

■ A galley-type Kitchen between the Breakfast Room and Dining Room

■ An optional basement, slab or crawl space foundation — please specify when ordering

MAIN AREA — 1,670 SQ. FT.

TOTAL LIVING AREA:
1,670 SQ. FT.

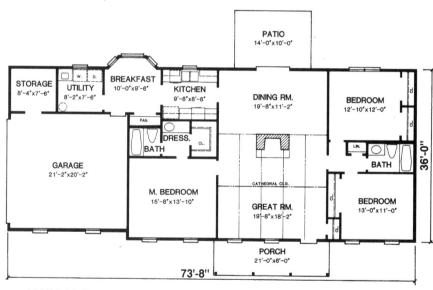

MAIN AREA

PRICE CODE A

PLENTY OF EXTERIOR INTEREST

No. 91063

■ This plan features:

— Three bedrooms

— Two full baths

■ Vaulted ceilings and an open interior creating a spacious feeling

■ A private Master Bedroom with a generous closet and Master Bath

■ Two additional bedrooms sharing the second full bath

■ A Kitchen with ample storage, countertops, and a built-in pantry

MAIN AREA — 1,207 SQ. FT.
GARAGE — 440 SQ. FT.

TOTAL LIVING AREA:
1,207 SQ. FT.

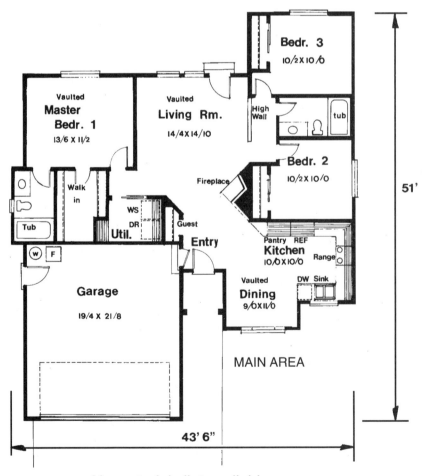

MAIN AREA

No materials list available

PRICE CODE B

VAULTED CEILINGS ADD SPACE

No. 92309

- This plan features:
- — Three bedrooms
- — Two full baths
- An covered entry leading into a tiled hall, the Kitchen/Dining Room, and the Great Room
- An oversized Great Room highlighted by a raised, hearth fireplace, built-in shelves, a vaulted ceiling and a sliding glass door to a Wood Deck
- An island cooktop Kitchen with a vaulted ceiling, offering laundry facilities and a decorative, box window in the Dining area
- A plush Master Suite with a double vanity bath and a walk-in closet
- Two additional bedrooms, one with a vaulted ceiling sharing a full hall bath

MAIN FLOOR — 1,544 SQ. FT.
GARAGE — 440 SQ. FT.

TOTAL LIVING AREA:
1,544 SQ. FT.

An
EXCLUSIVE DESIGN
By Gary Clayton

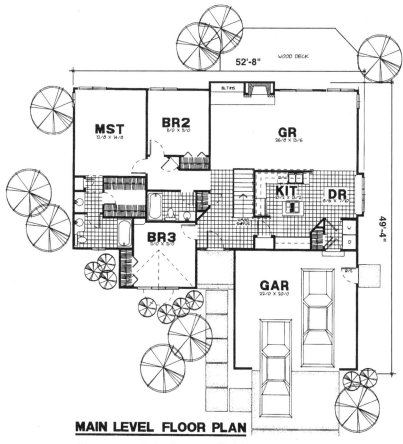

MAIN LEVEL FLOOR PLAN

No materials list available

PRICE CODE B

EXTERIOR ADDS DRAMA

No. 91349

- ■ This plan features:
- — Two bedrooms
- — Two full baths
- ■ A vaulted ceiling entry
- ■ A Living Room with a vaulted ceiling, accented by a bay window and an optional fireplace
- ■ A garden window, eating bar, and an abundance of storage space in the efficient Kitchen
- ■ A Master Bedroom with its own bath, a double sink vanity and a walk-in closet
- ■ A Library with a vaulted ceiling option and a window seat

MAIN AREA — 1,694 SQ. FT.

TOTAL LIVING AREA:
1,694 SQ. FT.

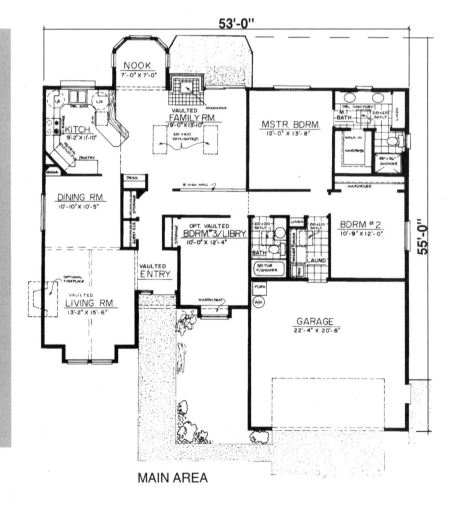

MAIN AREA

PRICE CODE B

COUNTRY STYLE AND CHARM

No. 91731

■ This plan features:

— Three bedrooms

— Two full baths

■ Brick accents, front facing gable, and railed wrap-around covered porch

■ A built-in range and oven in a dog-leg shaped Kitchen

■ A Nook with garage access for convenient unloading of groceries and other supplies

■ A bay window wrapping around the front of the formal Living Room

■ A Master Suite with French doors opening to the deck

MAIN AREA — 1,775 SQ. FT.
GARAGE — 681 SQ. FT.
WIDTH — 51'-6"
DEPTH — 65'-0"

**TOTAL LIVING AREA:
1,775 SQ. FT.**

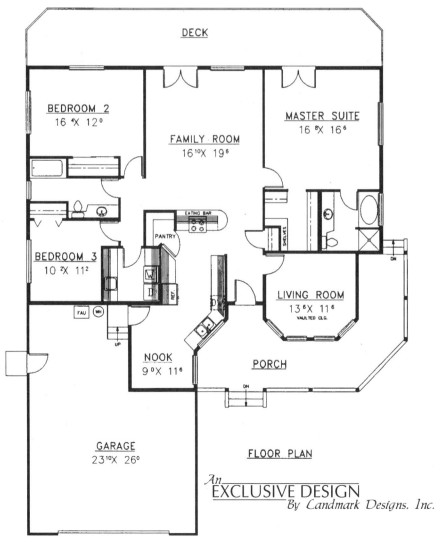

DECK

BEDROOM 2
16⁴X 12⁰

FAMILY ROOM
16¹⁰X 19⁶

MASTER SUITE
16⁶X 16⁶

EATING BAR

PANTRY

BEDROOM 3
10²X 11²

SHELVES

REF.

W

D

FAU

LIVING ROOM
13⁶X 11⁶
VAULTED CLG.

UP

NOOK
9⁰X 11⁶

PORCH

DN

GARAGE
23¹⁰X 26⁰

FLOOR PLAN

An EXCLUSIVE DESIGN
By Landmark Designs, Inc.

PRICE CODE A

*I*NEXPENSIVE RANCH DESIGN

No. 20062

■ This plan features:

— Three bedrooms

— Two full baths

■ A large picture window brightening the Breakfast area

■ A well planned Kitchen

■ A Living Room which is accented by an open beam across the sloping ceiling and wood burning fireplace

■ A Master Bedroom with an extremely large bath area

FIRST FLOOR — 1,500 SQ. FT.
BASEMENT — 1,500 SQ. FT.
GARAGE — 482 SQ. FT.

TOTAL LIVING AREA:
1,500 SQ. FT.

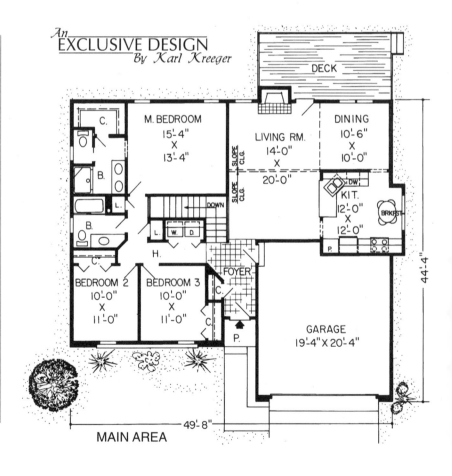

An
EXCLUSIVE DESIGN
By Karl Kreeger

PRICE CODE B

EXCITING CEILINGS ADD IMPACT

No. 20191

◼ This plan features:

— Three bedrooms

— Two full baths

◼ A brick hearth fireplace in the Living Room

◼ An efficient Kitchen, with an island and double sinks, that flows into the Dining Room, which features a decorative ceiling

◼ A private Master Suite with a decorative ceiling and a Master Bath

◼ Two additional bedrooms that share a full bath

MAIN AREA — 1,606 SQ. FT.
BASEMENT — 1,575 SQ. FT.
GARAGE — 545 SQ. FT.

TOTAL LIVING AREA:
1,606 SQ. FT.

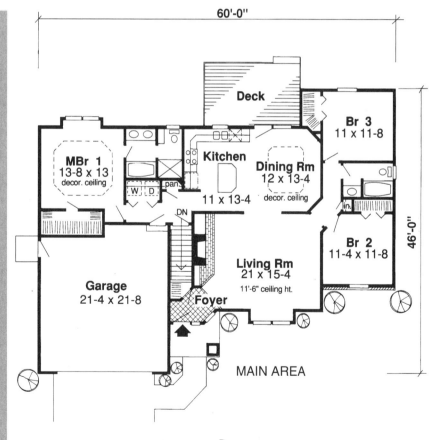

MAIN AREA

An
EXCLUSIVE DESIGN
By Karl Kreeger

PRICE CODE E

VAULTED SUNKEN LIVING ROOM

No. 90941

■ This plan features:

— Four bedrooms

— Two full and one half baths

■ A dramatic, sunken Living Room with a vaulted ceiling, fireplace, and glass walls to enjoy the view

■ A well-appointed, Kitchen with a peninsula counter and direct access to the Family Room, Dining Room or the sun deck

■ A Master Suite with a walk-in closet and a private full bath

■ A Family Room with direct access to the rear sun deck

FIRST FLOOR — 1,464 SQ. FT.
BASEMENT FLOOR— 1,187 SQ. FT.
GARAGE — 418 SQ. FT.

TOTAL LIVING AREA:
2,651 SQ. FT.

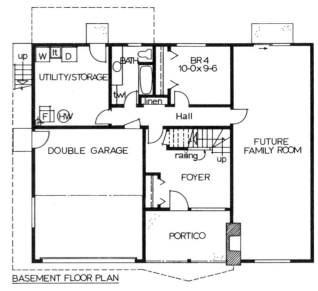

BASEMENT FLOOR PLAN

MAIN FLOOR PLAN

An
EXCLUSIVE DESIGN
By Westhome Planners, Ltd.

PRICE CODE C

L-SHAPED BUNGALOW WITH TWO PORCHES

No. 90407

■ This plan features:

— Three bedrooms

— Two full baths

■ A Master Suite with a lavish Master Bath including a garden tub, shower, his-n-her vanities and separate walk-in closets

■ Two additional bedrooms having ample closet space and sharing a full hall bath

■ A large Family Room accentuated by a fireplace

■ A U-shaped Kitchen with a built-in pantry, double sink and ample storage and counter space

■ A sunny, bay Breakfast Nook for informal eating

■ An optional basement, slab or crawl space foundation — please specify when ordering

FIRST FLOOR — 1,950 SQ. FT.

**TOTAL LIVING AREA:
1,950 SQ. FT.**

MAIN AREA

PRICE CODE B

LIGHT AND AIRY DESIGN

No. 10745

■ This plan features:

— Three bedrooms

— Two full baths

■ An open plan with cathedral ceilings

■ A fireplaced Great Room flowing into the Dining Room

■ A Master Bedroom with a private Master Bath

■ An efficient Kitchen, with Laundry area and pantry in close proximity

MAIN AREA — 1,643 SQ. FT.
BASEMENT — 1,643 SQ. FT.
GARAGE — 484 SQ. FT.

TOTAL LIVING AREA:
1,643 SQ. FT.

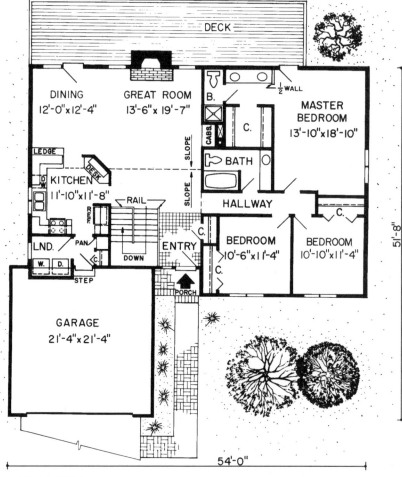

MAIN AREA

PRICE CODE A

RANCH PROVIDES GREAT KITCHEN AREA

No. 34054

■ This plan features:

— Three bedrooms

— Two full baths

■ A Dining Room with sliding glass doors to the backyard

■ Access to the Garage through the laundry room

■ A Master Bedroom with a private full bath

■ An two-car Garage

FIRST FLOOR — 1,400 SQ. FT.
BASEMENT — 1,400 SQ. FT.
GARAGE — 528 SQ. FT.

TOTAL LIVING AREA:
1,400 SQ. FT.

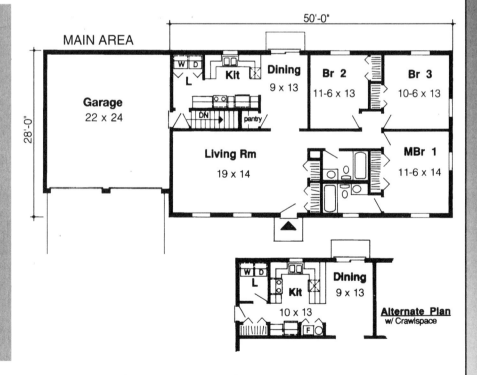

PRICE CODE B

GRACEFUL PORCH ENHANCES CHARM

No. 90106

■ This plan features:

— Three bedrooms

— Two full baths

■ A formal Living Room sheltered by a railed porch

■ A hobby area including laundry facilities

■ A Kitchen, Dining, and Family Room in a "three in one" design

■ An optional basement, slab or crawl space foundation — please specify when ordering

MAIN AREA — 1,643 SQ. FT.

TOTAL LIVING AREA:
1,643 SQ. FT.

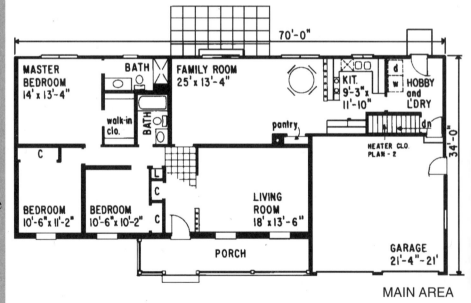

MAIN AREA

PRICE CODE A

DETAILED RANCH DESIGN

No. 90360

■ This plan features:

— Three bedrooms

— Two full baths

■ A Breakfast area with a vaulted ceiling and access to the deck

■ An efficient Kitchen with built-in pantry and appliances

■ A Master bedroom with private bath and ample closet space

■ A large Great Room with a vaulted ceiling and cozy fireplace

MAIN AREA — 1,283 SQ. FT.

TOTAL LIVING AREA:
1,283 SQ. FT.

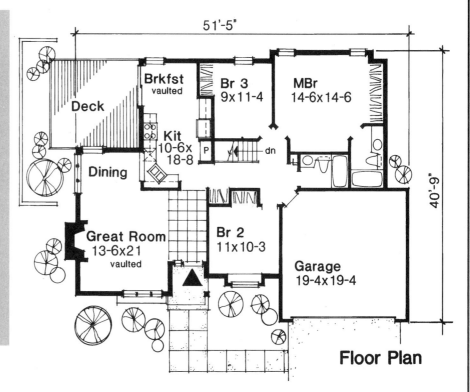

Floor Plan

PRICE CODE A

CATHEDRAL CEILING IN LIVING ROOM AND MASTER SUITE

No. 24402

■ This plan features:

— Three bedrooms

— Two full baths

■ A spacious Living Room with a cathedral ceiling and elegant fireplace

■ A Dining Room that adjoins both the Living Room and the Kitchen

■ An efficient Kitchen, with double sinks, ample cabinet space and peninsula counter that doubles as an eating bar

■ A convenient hallway laundry center

■ A Master Suite with a cathedral ceiling and a private Master Bath

MAIN AREA — 1,346 SQ. FT.
GARAGE — 449 SQ. FT.

TOTAL LIVING AREA:
1,346 SQ. FT.

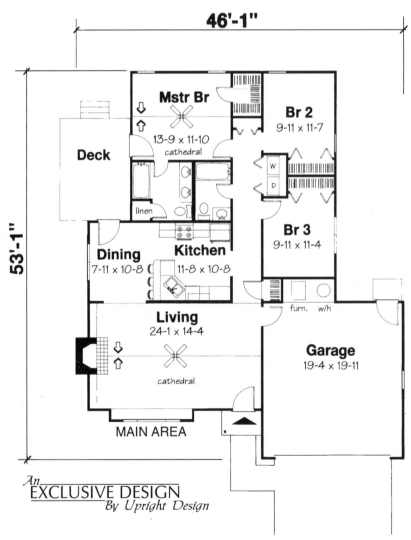

An
EXCLUSIVE DESIGN
By Upright Design

No materials list available

PRICE CODE B

PLENTY OF NATURAL LIGHT

No. 24317

■ This plan features:

— Three bedrooms

— Two full baths

■ A generous use of windows throughout the home, creating a bright living space

■ A center work island and a built-in pantry in the Kitchen

■ A sunny Eating Nook for informal eating and a formal Dining Room for entertaining

■ A large Living Room, with a cozy fireplace to add atmosphere to the room as well as warmth

■ A Master Bedroom with a private bath and double closets

■ Two additional bedrooms that share a full, compartmented hall bath

MAIN AREA — 1,620 SQ. FT.

TOTAL LIVING AREA:
1,620 SQ. FT.

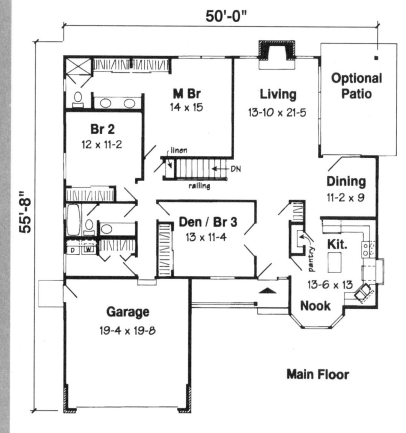

50'-0"

55'-8"

Optional Patio

M Br
14 x 15

Living
13-10 x 21-5

Br 2
12 x 11-2

linen

DN

railing

Dining
11-2 x 9

Den / Br 3
13 x 11-4

Kit.

D W

pantry

13-6 x 13

Garage
19-4 x 19-8

Nook

Main Floor

An
EXCLUSIVE DESIGN
By Marshall Associates

PRICE CODE A

VACATION PLAN HAS WELL ORGANIZED LAYOUT

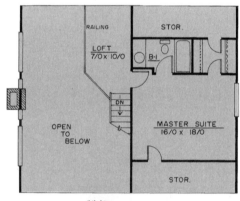

UPPER FLOOR

No. 91033

■ This plan features:

— Two bedrooms

— Two full baths

■ A two-story Living Room and Dining Room with a handsome stone fireplace

■ A well-appointed Kitchen with a peninsula counter

■ A Master Suite with a walk-in closet and private Master Bath

■ A large utility room with laundry facilities

■ An optional basement or crawl space foundation — please specify when ordering

FIRST FLOOR — 952 SQ. FT.
SECOND FLOOR — 297 SQ. FT.

TOTAL LIVING AREA: 1,249 SQ. FT.

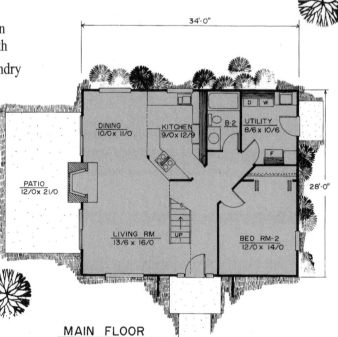

MAIN FLOOR

PRICE CODE B

ATTRACTIVE SLOPED CEILING FEATURED IN RANCH DESIGN

No. 10548

- ■ This plan features:
- — Three bedrooms
- — Two and one half baths
- ■ A fireplace and sloped ceiling in the Living Room
- ■ A Master Bedroom complete with a full bath, shower and dressing area
- ■ A decorative ceiling in the Dining Room

MAIN AREA — 1,688 SQ. FT.
BASEMENT — 1,688 SQ. FT.
SCREENED PORCH — 120 SQ. FT.
GARAGE — 489 SQ. FT.

TOTAL LIVING AREA:
1,688 SQ. FT.

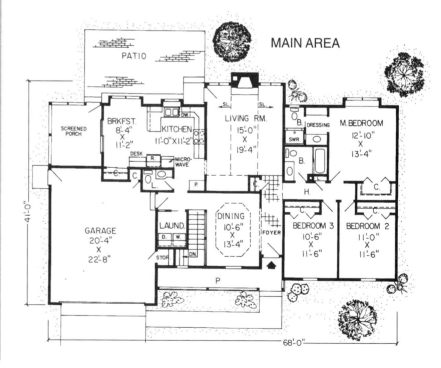

An
EXCLUSIVE DESIGN
By Karl Kreeger

PRICE CODE B

CASUAL LIVING INSIDE AND OUT

No. 92703

■ This plan features:

— Three bedrooms

— Two full baths

■ A Living Room with a ten foot ceiling and a cozy corner fireplace

■ An enormous Dining Area that is able to handle even the largest family dinners

■ A large rear Porch that is perfect for outdoor dining

■ A conveniently placed Laundry Room

■ His-n-her walk-in closets and a double vanity in the Master Bath

■ Secondary bedrooms that share a full hall bath with a double vanity

MAIN AREA — 1,772 SQ. FT.

TOTAL LIVING AREA:
1,772 SQ. FT.

No materials list available

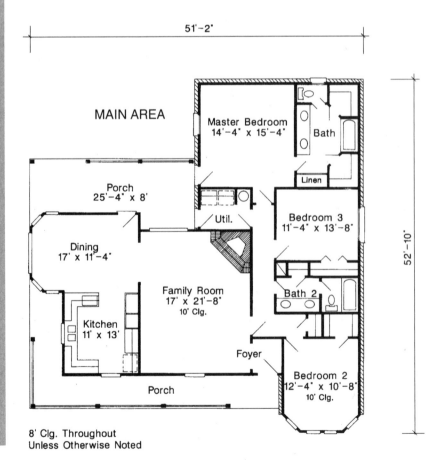

8' Clg. Throughout
Unless Otherwise Noted

PRICE CODE A

QUAINT STARTER HOME

No. 92400

■ This plan features:

— Three bedrooms

— Two full baths

■ A vaulted ceiling giving an airy feeling to the Dining and Living Rooms

■ A streamlined Kitchen with a comfortable work area, a double sink and ample cabinet space

■ A cozy fireplace in the Living Room

■ A Master Suite with a large closet, French doors leading to the patio and a private bath

■ Two additional bedrooms sharing a full bath

MAIN AREA — 1,050 SQ. FT.

TOTAL LIVING AREA:
1,050 SQ. FT.

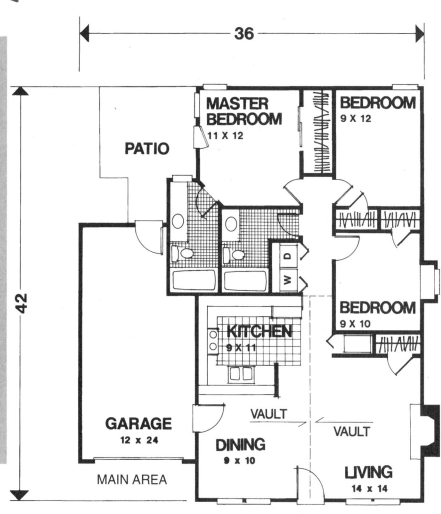

36

42

PATIO

MASTER BEDROOM
11 X 12

BEDROOM
9 X 12

BEDROOM
9 X 10

KITCHEN
9 X 11

GARAGE
12 x 24

DINING
9 x 10

VAULT

VAULT

LIVING
14 x 14

MAIN AREA

W   D

No materials list available

PRICE CODE A

ELEGANT WINDOW TREATMENTS

No. 34150

■ This plan features:

— Two bedrooms (optional third)

— Two full baths

■ A huge, arched window that floods the front room with natural light

■ A homey, well-lit Office or Den

■ Compact, efficient use of space

■ An efficient Kitchen with easy access to the Dining Room

■ A fireplaced Living Room with a sloping ceiling and a window wall

■ A Master Bedroom sporting a private Master Bath with a roomy walk-in closet

FIRST FLOOR — 1,492 SQ. FT.
BASEMENT — 1,486 SQ. FT.
GARAGE — 462 SQ. FT.

TOTAL LIVING AREA:
1,492 SQ. FT.

An
EXCLUSIVE DESIGN
By Karl Kreeger

FOUNDATION
OPTION

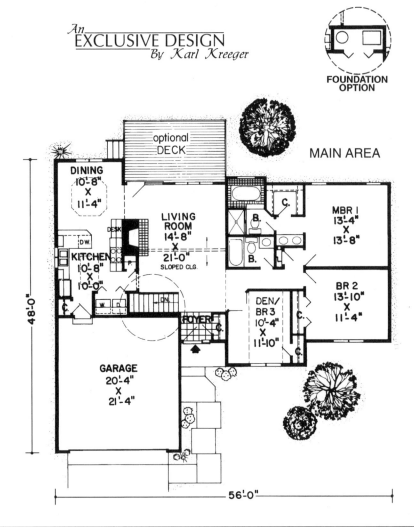

PRICE CODE A

ARCHED WINDOW ENHANCES FACADE

No. 99345

■ This plan features:

— Three bedrooms

— Two full baths

■ A Great Room and Dining area with vaulted ceilings

■ A Great Room with a fabulous fireplace

■ A Kitchen and sunny Breakfast area with access to a rear deck

■ A Master Suite with a private full bath and one wall of closet space

MAIN AREA — 1,325 SQ. FT.

TOTAL LIVING AREA:
1,325 SQ. FT.

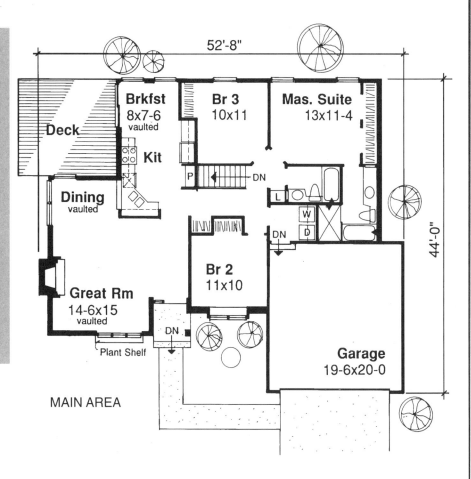

52'-8"

Deck

Brkfst
8x7-6
vaulted

Kit

Dining
vaulted

Great Rm
14-6x15
vaulted

Plant Shelf

Br 3
10x11

Mas. Suite
13x11-4

P

DN

L

W
D

DN

Br 2
11x10

DN

44'-0"

Garage
19-6x20-0

MAIN AREA

PRICE CODE C

COZY TRADITIONAL WITH STYLE

No. 99208

■ This plan features:

— Three bedrooms

— Two full baths

■ A convenient one-level design

■ A galley-style Kitchen that shares a snack bar with the spacious Gathering Room

■ A focal point fireplace making the Gathering Room warm and inviting

■ An ample Master Suite with a luxury Bath which includes a whirlpool tub and separate Dressing Room

■ Two additional bedrooms, one that could double as a Study, located at the front of the house

FIRST FLOOR — 1,830 SQ. FT.
BASEMENT — 1,830 SQ. FT.

TOTAL LIVING AREA:
1,830 SQ. FT.

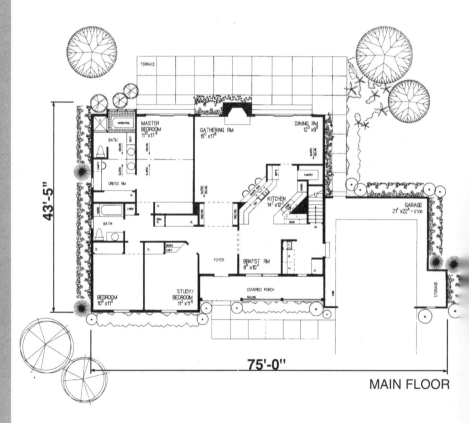

MAIN FLOOR

PRICE CODE A

COUNTRY RANCH

No. 91797

- This plan features:
- — Three bedrooms
- — Two full baths
- A railed and covered wrap-around porch, adding charm to this country-styled home
- A high vaulted ceiling in the Living Room
- A smaller Kitchen with ample cupboard and counter space, that is augmented by a large pantry
- An informal Family Room with access to the wood deck
- A private Master Suite with a spa tub and a walk-in closet
- Two family bedrooms that share a full hall bath
- A shop and storage area in the two-car garage

MAIN AREA — 1,485 SQ. FT.
GARAGE — 701 SQ. FT.
WIDTH — 63'-0"
DEPTH — 51'-6"

TOTAL LIVING AREA:
1,485 SQ. FT.

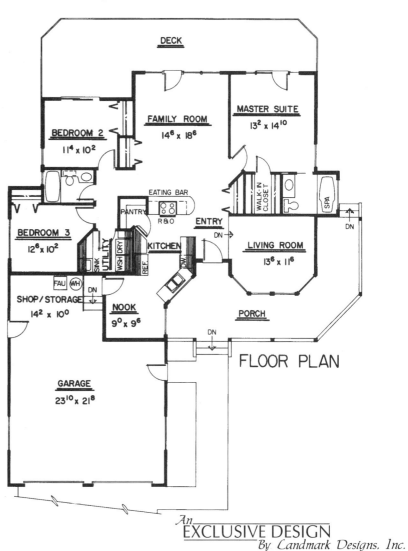

FLOOR PLAN

An
EXCLUSIVE DESIGN
By Landmark Designs, Inc.

PRICE CODE C

MODERATE RANCH WITH EXCITING FEATURES

No. 90441

■ This plan features:

— Three bedrooms

— Two full baths

■ A large Great Room with a vaulted ceiling and a stone fireplace with bookshelves on either side

■ A spacious Kitchen with ample cabinet space, conveniently located next to the large Dining Room

■ A Master Suite having a large bath with a garden tub, double vanity and a walk-in closet

■ Two other large bedrooms, each with a walk-in closet and access to the full bath

■ An optional basement, slab or crawl space foundation — please specify when ordering

MAIN AREA — 1,811 SQ. FT.

TOTAL LIVING AREA:
1,811 SQ. FT.

MAIN AREA

PRICE CODE A

*A*NOTHER NICE RANCH DESIGN

No. 90354

■ This plan features:

— Three bedrooms

— Two full baths

■ A vaulted ceiling in the Great Room that includes a fireplace and access to the rear deck

■ Double door entrance into the Den/third bedroom

■ A Kitchen and breakfast area with a vaulted ceiling and an efficient layout

■ A Master Suite crowned by a vaulted ceiling, and pampered by a private bath and dressing area

■ A full hall bath that serves the two additional bedrooms

MAIN AREA — 1,360 SQ. FT.

**TOTAL LIVING AREA:
1,360 SQ. FT.**

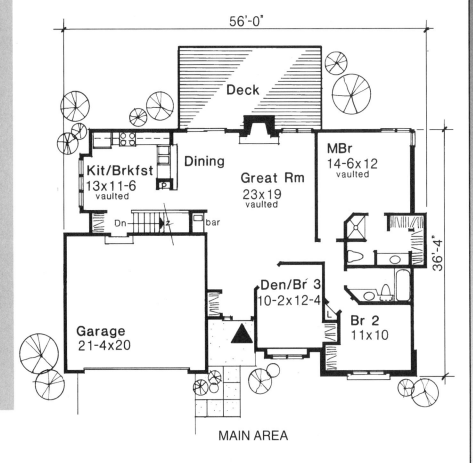

MAIN AREA

PRICE CODE B

ANGLED CONTEMPORARY

No. 99633

■ This plan features:

— Three bedrooms

— Two full and one half baths

■ An angled shape that allows the house to be rotated on a site to give optimum orientation

■ A spacious Foyer that opens to the Living Room

■ A heat-circulating fireplace in the Living Room

■ Sliding glass doors in the Living Room and the Dining Room that lead to a partially covered terrace

■ A cathedral ceiling in the Family Room which also has a heat-circulating fireplace

■ A Master Suite with a cathedral ceiling and private bath with double vanity and whirlpool tub

■ Two additional bedrooms share a full hall bath with a double vanity and whirlpool tub

MAIN AREA — 1,798 SQ. FT.
BASEMENT — 1,715 SQ. FT.
GARAGE — 456 SQ. FT.

TOTAL LIVING AREA:
1,798 SQ. FT.

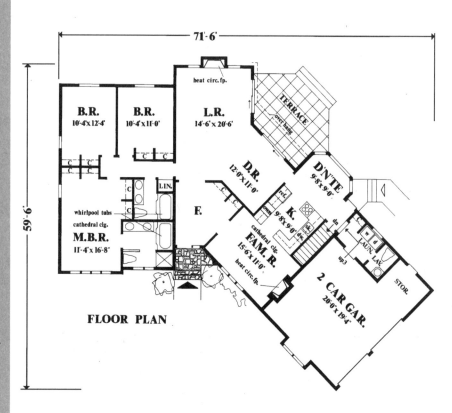

FLOOR PLAN

PRICE CODE B

COUNTRY CHARM

No. 99635

■ This plan features:

— Three bedrooms

— Two and one half baths

■ A large heat-circulating fireplace

■ A Master Bedroom with a private bath including a separate stall shower and whirlpool tub

■ A comfortable lifestyle by separating the formal and informal areas

■ Access to the Garage through the mudroom, which contains laundry facilities and extra closet space

MAIN AREA — 1,650 SQ. FT.
GARAGE — 491 SQ. FT.

TOTAL LIVING AREA:
1,650 SQ. FT.

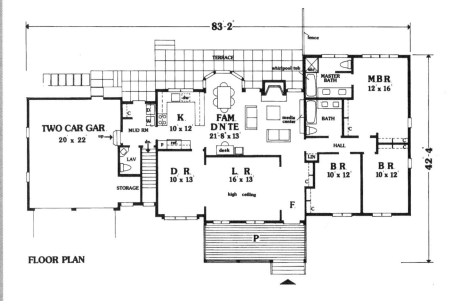

FLOOR PLAN

PRICE CODE D

Brick Design Has Striking Exterior

No. 10549

■ This plan features:

— Three bedrooms

— Three full and one half baths

■ A circle-head window that sets off a striking exterior

■ A Master Bedroom including a sloping ceiling, large closet space, and a private bath with both a tub and shower

■ A Great Room with impressive open-crossed beams and a wood-burning fireplace

■ A Kitchen with access to the Dining Room and Breakfast Room

FIRST FLOOR — 2,280 SQ. FT.
BASEMENT — 2,280 SQ. FT.
GARAGE — 528 SQ. FT.

TOTAL LIVING AREA:
2,280 SQ. FT.

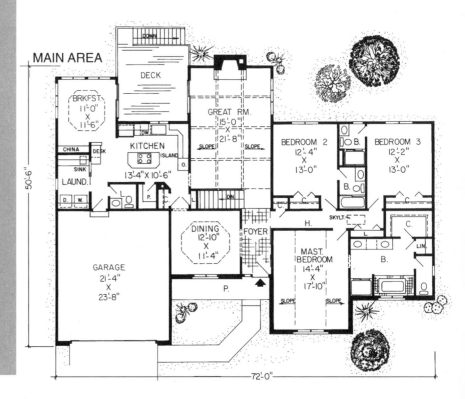

An
EXCLUSIVE DESIGN
By Karl Kreeger

PRICE CODE B

COMPACT AND APPEALING

No. 20075

■ This plan features:

— Three bedrooms

— Two full baths

■ A fireplaced Living Room and formal Dining Room with extra wide doorways

■ A centrally-located Kitchen for maximum convenience

■ A Master Bedroom with a vaulted ceiling and a private Master Bath and walk-in closet

MAIN AREA — 1,682 SQ. FT.
BASEMENT — 1,682 SQ. FT.
GARAGE — 484 SQ. FT.

TOTAL LIVING AREA:
1,682 SQ. FT.

An
EXCLUSIVE DESIGN
By Karl Kreeger

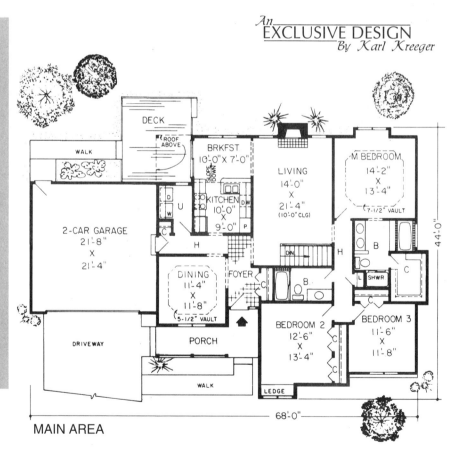

MAIN AREA

PRICE CODE B

WINDOW BOXES ADD ROMANTIC CHARM

No. 90684

■ This plan features:

— Three bedrooms

— Two full and one half baths

■ A spacious Living Room and formal Dining Room combination that is perfect for entertaining

■ A Family Room with a large fireplace and an expansive glass wall that overlooks the patio

■ An informal Dining bay, convenient to both the Kitchen and the Family Room

■ An efficient and well-equipped Kitchen, with a peninsula counter dividing it from the Family Room

■ A Master Bedroom with his-n-her closets and a private Master Bath

MAIN AREA — 1,590 SQ. FT.
BASEMENT — 900 SQ. FT.

TOTAL LIVING AREA:
1,590 SQ. FT.

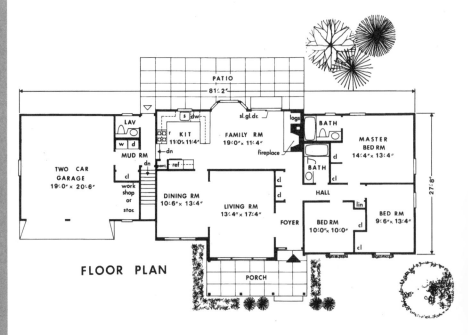

FLOOR PLAN

PRICE CODE A

EXPANSIVE, NOT EXPENSIVE

No. 90623

■ This plan features:

— Three bedrooms

— Two full baths

■ A Master Suite with his and her closets and a private Master Bath

■ Two additional bedrooms that share a full hall closet

■ A pleasant Dining Room that overlooks a rear garden

■ A well-equipped Kitchen with a built-in planning corner and eat-in space

■ A basement foundation only

FIRST FLOOR — 1,474 SQ. FT.

TOTAL LIVING AREA:
1,474 SQ. FT.

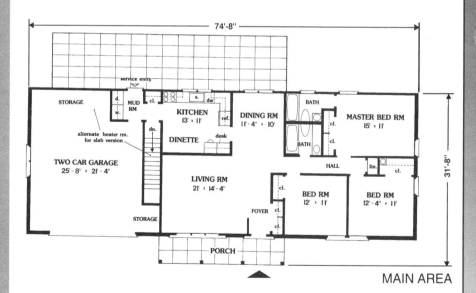

74'-8"

31'-8"

STORAGE

service entry

MUD RM

KITCHEN
13' x 11'

DINING RM
11'-4" x 10'

BATH

BATH

MASTER BED RM
15' x 11'

alternate heater rm. for slab version

DINETTE

desk

TWO CAR GARAGE
25'-8" x 21'-4"

dn.

LIVING RM
21' x 14'-4"

HALL

lin.

cl.

STORAGE

FOYER

cl.

BED RM
12' x 11'

BED RM
12'-4" x 11'

PORCH

MAIN AREA

PRICE CODE B

INTERIOR AND EXTERIOR UNITY DISTINGUISHES PLAN

No. 90398

■ This plan features:

— Three bedrooms

— Two full baths

■ A vaulted ceiling Living Room with cozy fireplace

■ Columns dividing the Living and Dining Rooms, and half-walls separating the Kitchen and Breakfast Room

■ A luxurious Master Suite with a private sky-lit bath, double vanities and a generous walk-in closet

MAIN AREA —1,630 SQ. FT.

TOTAL LIVING AREA:
1,630 SQ. FT.

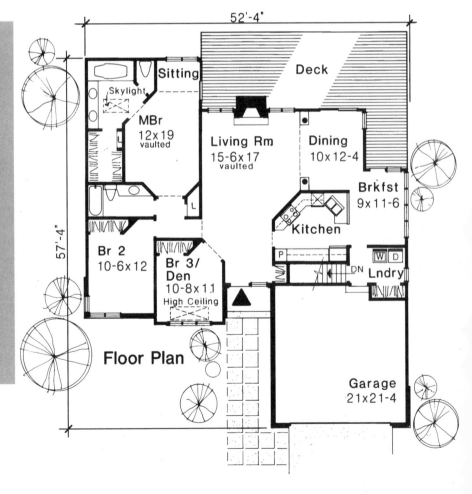

Floor Plan

PRICE CODE A

PERFECT FIRST HOME

No. 92704

■ This plan features:

— Three bedrooms

— Two full baths

■ A front porch with turned posts and railing, and a corner box window

■ A large Living Room with an 11 foot ceiling, sloping towards the sliding glass doors to the rear yard

■ A cathedral ceiling in the Dining Area, with a view of the porch through an elegant window

■ A corner double sink below the corner box window in the efficient Kitchen

■ A secluded Master Bedroom that includes a private bath and a walk-in closet

■ Two additional bedrooms that share a full hall bath

MAIN AREA — 1,078 SQ. FT.
GARAGE — 431 SQ. FT.

TOTAL LIVING AREA:
1,078 SQ. FT.

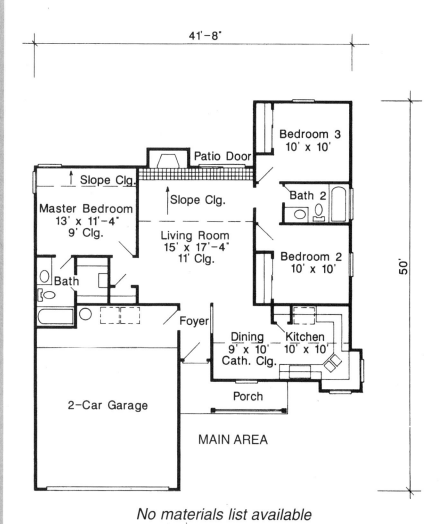

No materials list available

PRICE CODE A

NOSTALGIA RETURNS

No. 99321

■ This plan features:

— Three bedrooms

— Two full baths

■ A half-round transom window with quarter-round detail and a vaulted ceiling in the Great Room

■ A cozy corner fireplace which brings warmth to the Great Room

■ A vaulted ceiling in the Kitchen/Breakfast area

■ A Master Suite with a walk-in closet and a private Master Bath

■ Two additional bedrooms which share a full hall bath

MAIN AREA — 1,368 SQ. FT.

TOTAL LIVING AREA:
1,368 SQ. FT.

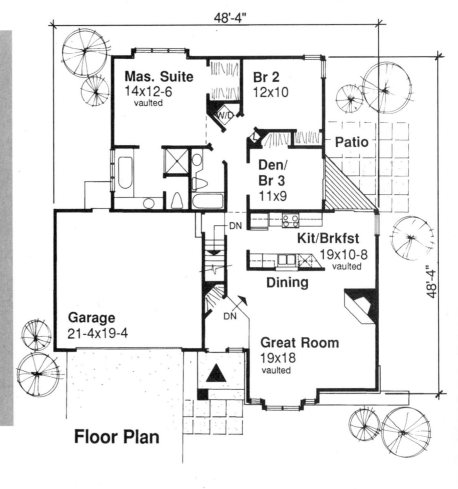

Floor Plan

PRICE CODE A

ONE STORY COUNTRY HOME

No. 99639

■ This plan features:

— Three bedrooms

— Two full baths

■ A Living Room with an imposing, high ceiling that slopes down to a normal height of eight feet, focusing on the decorative heat-circulating fireplace at the rear wall

■ An efficient Kitchen that adjoins the Dining Room that views the front Porch

■ A Dinette Area for informal eating in the Kitchen that can comfortably seat six people

■ A Master Suite arranged with a large dressing area that has a walk-in closet plus two linear closets and space for a vanity

■ Two family bedrooms that share a full hall bath

MAIN AREA — 1,367 SQ. FT.
BASEMENT — 1,267 SQ. FT.
GARAGE — 431 SQ. FT.

TOTAL LIVING AREA:
1,367 SQ. FT.

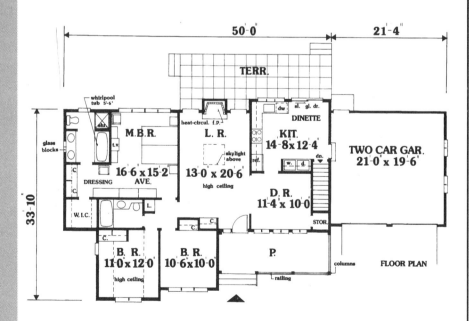

PRICE CODE A

CAREFREE COMFORT

No. 90692

■ This plan features:

— Three bedrooms

— Two full baths

■ Cedar shingle siding and flower boxes

■ A heat-circulating fireplace

■ A central Foyer separating active areas from the bedroom wing

■ A sunny Living Room with an arched window, fireplace, and soaring cathedral ceilings

■ A formal Dining Room adjoining the Living Room

MAIN AREA — 1,492 SQ. FT.

TOTAL LIVING AREA: 1,492 SQ. FT.

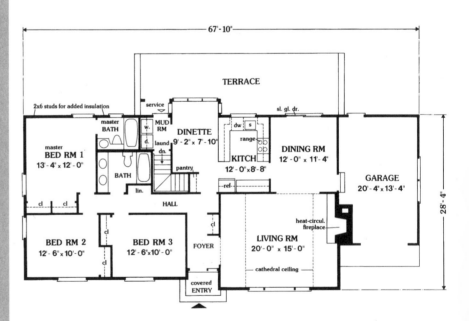

FLOOR PLAN

PRICE CODE A

SOARING CEILINGS ADD SPACE AND DRAMA

No. 90288

■ This plan features:

— Two bedrooms (with optional third bedroom)

— Two full baths

■ A sunny Master Suite with a sloping ceiling, private terrace entry, and luxurious garden bath with an adjoining Dressing Room

■ A Gathering Room with a fireplace, study and formal Dining Room, flowing together for a more spacious feeling

■ A convenient pass-through that adds to the efficiency of the galley Kitchen and adjoining Breakfast Room

MAIN AREA — 1,387 SQ. FT.

TOTAL LIVING AREA:
1,387 SQ. FT.

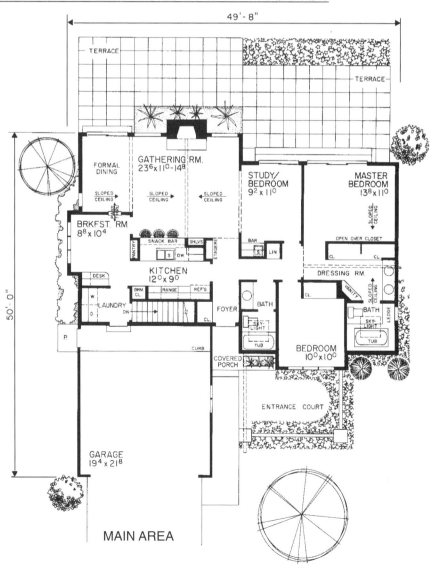

MAIN AREA

PRICE CODE B

PRIVATE MASTER BEDROOM SUITE

No. 20104

■ This plan features:

— Three bedrooms

— Two full baths

■ A sky-lit Kitchen

■ Ample closet space

■ Built-in storage areas in the Kitchen

■ A Master bath with twin vanities, a raised tub, and a walk-in shower

MAIN AREA — 1,686 SQ. FT.
BASEMENT — 1,677 SQ. FT.
GARAGE — 475 SQ. FT.

TOTAL LIVING AREA:
1,686 SQ. FT.

An
EXCLUSIVE DESIGN
By Karl Kreeger

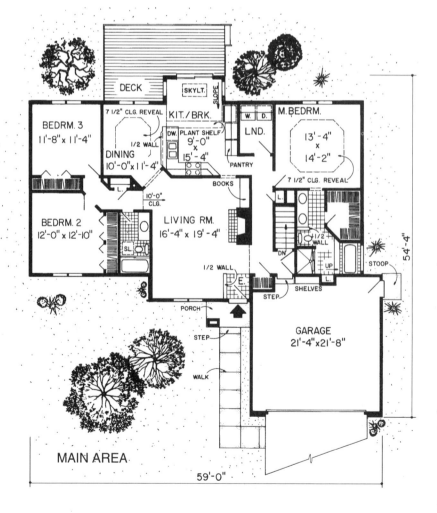

PRICE CODE B

ABUNDANCE OF CLOSET SPACE

No. 20204

■ This plan features:

— Three bedrooms

— Two full baths

■ Roomy walk-in closets in all the bedrooms

■ A Master Bedroom with decorative ceiling and a private full bath

■ A fireplaced Living Room with sloped ceilings and sliders to the deck

■ An efficient Kitchen with plenty of cupboard space and a pantry

MAIN AREA —1,532 SQ. FT.
GARAGE — 484 SQ. FT.

TOTAL LIVING AREA:
1,532 SQ. FT.

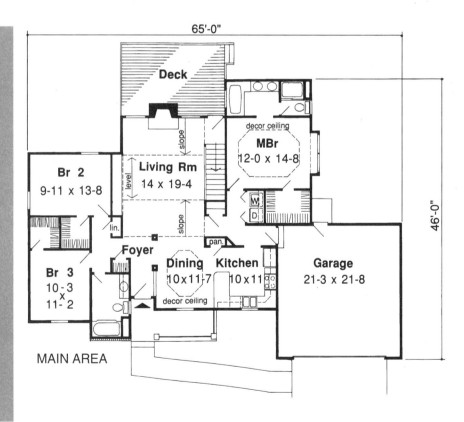

An
EXCLUSIVE DESIGN
By Karl Kreeger

PRICE CODE B

FOYER ISOLATES BEDROOM WING

No. 20087

- ■ This plan features:
- — Three bedrooms
- — Two full baths
- ■ A Living Room complete with a window wall, flanking a massive fireplace
- ■ A Dining Room with recessed ceilings and a pass-through for convenience
- ■ A Master Suite tucked behind the two-car garage for maximum noise protection
- ■ A spacious Kitchen with built-ins and access to the two-car garage

MAIN AREA —1,568 SQ. FT.
BASEMENT — 1,568 SQ. FT.
GARAGE — 484 SQ. FT.

TOTAL LIVING AREA:
1,568 SQ. FT.

An
EXCLUSIVE DESIGN
By Karl Kreeger

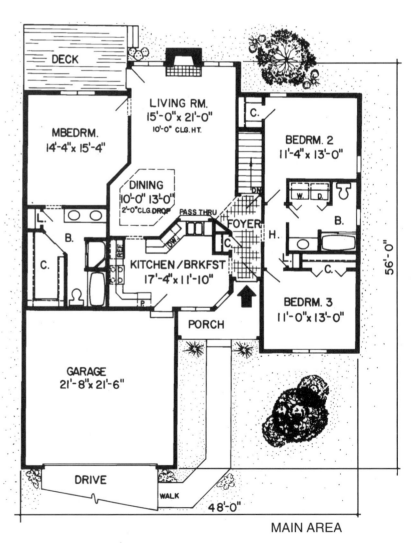

MAIN AREA

PRICE CODE B

RANCH PROVIDES GREAT FLOOR PLAN

No. 34055

■ This plan features:

— Four bedrooms

— Two full baths

■ A large Living Room and Dining Room, flowing together into one open space for perfect entertaining

■ A Laundry area, which doubles as a mudroom, off the Kitchen

■ A Master Suite including a private bath

■ A two-car Garage

MAIN AREA — 1,527 SQ. FT.
BASEMENT — 1,344 SQ. FT.
GARAGE — 425 SQ. FT.

**TOTAL LIVING AREA:
1,527 SQ. FT.**

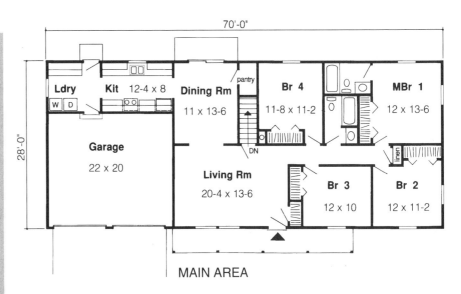

MAIN AREA

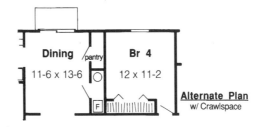

Alternate Plan
w/ Crawlspace

PRICE CODE A

AFFORDABLE LIVING

No. 24303

■ This plan features:

— Three bedrooms

— Two full baths

■ A sheltered entrance into a roomy Living Room, graced with a large front window

■ A formal Dining Room flowing from the Living Room, allowing for ease in entertaining

■ A well-appointed U-shaped Kitchen with double sinks and adequate storage

■ A Master Bedroom equipped with a full Bath

■ Two additional bedrooms that share a full hall bath complete with a convenient laundry center

■ A covered Patio, tucked behind the garage, perfect for a cook out or picnic

MAIN AREA — 984 SQ. FT.
BASEMENT — 960 SQ. FT.
GARAGE — 280 SQ. FT.
OPT. 2-CAR GARAGE — 400 SQ. FT.

TOTAL LIVING AREA:
984 SQ. FT.

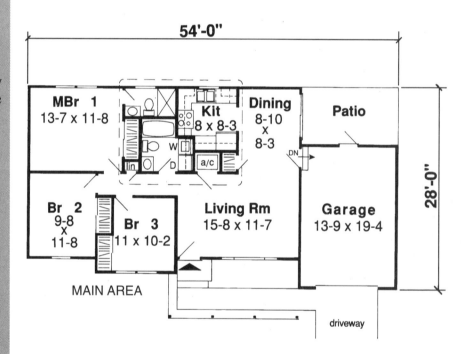

MAIN AREA

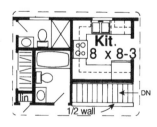

Basement Option

An
EXCLUSIVE DESIGN
By Marshall Associates

PRICE CODE A

CHAMPAGNE STYLE ON A SODA-POP BUDGET

No. 24302

■ This plan features:

— Three bedrooms

— Two full baths

■ Multiple gables, circle-top windows, and a unique exterior setting this delightful Ranch apart in any neighborhood

■ Living and Dining Rooms flowing together to create a very roomy feeling

■ Sliding doors leading from the Dining Room to a covered patio

■ A Master Bedroom with a private Bath

MAIN AREA — 988 SQ. FT.
BASEMENT — 988 SQ. FT.
GARAGE — 280 SQ. FT
OPTIONAL 2-CAR GARAGE — 384 SQ. FT.

TOTAL LIVING AREA: 988 SQ. FT.

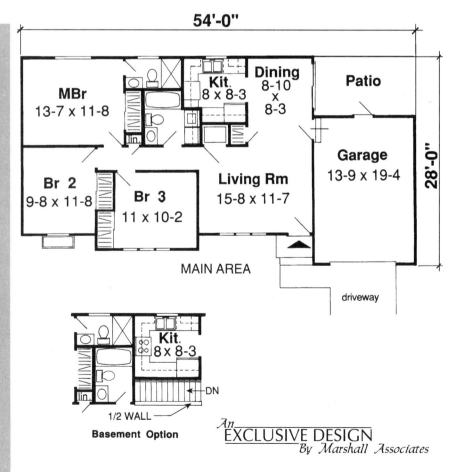

An
EXCLUSIVE DESIGN
By Marshall Associates

PRICE CODE A

CAPTIVATING SUN-CATCHER

No. 99303

■ This plan features:

— Two bedrooms

— Two full baths

■ A glass-walled Breakfast Room adjoining the vaulted-ceiling Kitchen

■ A fireplaced, vaulted ceiling Living Room that flows from the Dining Room

■ A greenhouse window over the tub in the luxurious Master Bath

■ Two walk-in closets and glass sliders in the Master Bedroom

MAIN AREA — 1,421 SQ. FT.

TOTAL LIVING AREA: 1,421 SQ. FT.

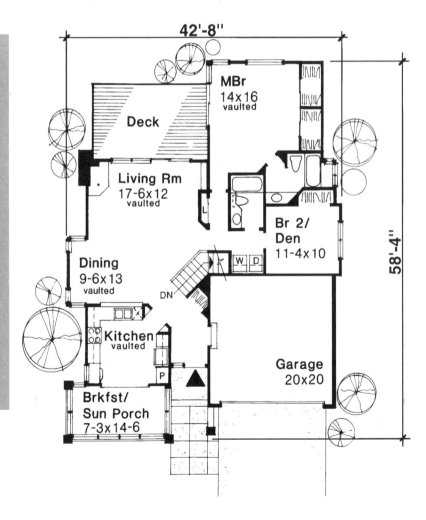

PRICE CODE B

EASY ONE FLOOR LIVING

No. 99216

■ This plan features:

— Three bedrooms

— Two full baths

■ Living areas conveniently grouped in the right half of the home for everyday activities

■ A Gathering Room with a sloped ceiling and a fireplace

■ A Kitchen designed for easy cooking with a closet pantry, plenty of counter space, and cupboards

■ A third bedroom making a perfect home office or study

MAIN AREA — 1,521 SQ. FT.
BASEMENT — 1,521 SQ. FT.

**TOTAL LIVING AREA:
1,521 SQ. FT.**

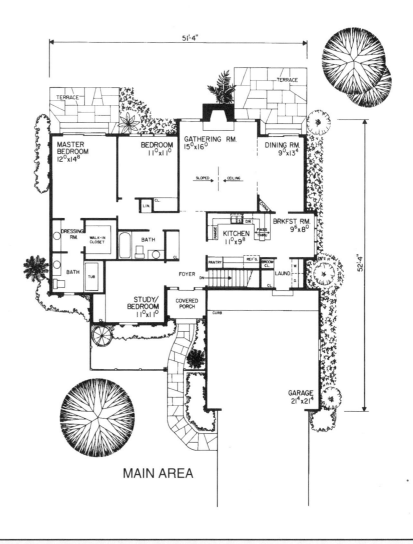

MAIN AREA

PRICE CODE A

DESIGNED FOR INFORMAL LIFE STYLE

No. 90325

■ This plan features:

— Two bedrooms

— One full bath

■ A Great Room and Kitchen accented by vaulted ceilings

■ A conveniently arranged L-shaped food preparation center

■ A Dining Room overlooking a deck through sliding doors

■ A Great Room highlighted by a corner fireplace

■ A Master Bedroom including a separate vanity and dressing area

FIRST FLOOR — 988 SQ. FT.
BASEMENT — 988 SQ. FT.
GARAGE — 400 SQ. FT.

TOTAL LIVING AREA:
988 SQ. FT.

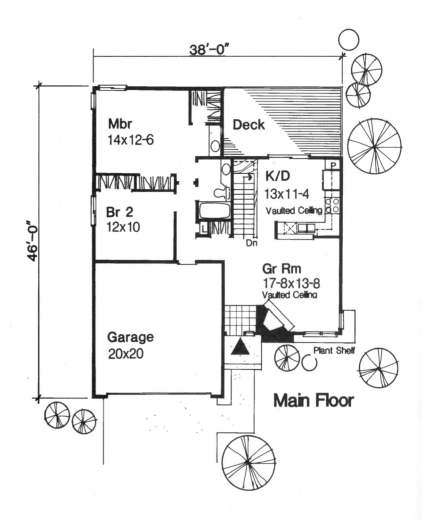

PRICE CODE A

OPEN LIVING AREA, PLUS TRADITIONAL STYLING

No. 90107

- ■ This plan features:
- — Two bedrooms
- — Two full baths
- ■ A Great Room concept that combines the Kitchen, Dining and Living Rooms
- ■ An efficient U-shaped Kitchen, equipped with a double sink and plenty of cupboard and counter space
- ■ A Dining Room that has direct access to the rear patio, expanding living spaces in warmer months
- ■ A Master Bedroom with a walk-in closet and a private bath
- ■ A second bedroom that has use of the full hall bath
- ■ A two-car garage with plenty of storage space
- ■ An optional basement, slab or crawl space foundation — please specify when ordering

MAIN AREA — 1,092 SQ. FT.

TOTAL LIVING AREA:
1,092 SQ. FT.

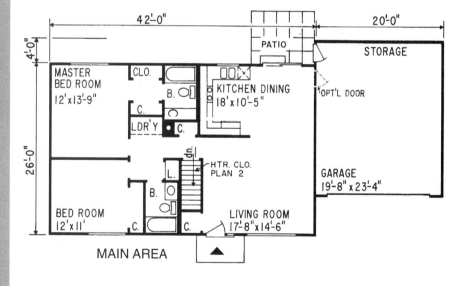

42'-0" 20'-0"

PATIO STORAGE

4'-0"

MASTER BED ROOM 12'x13'-9" CLO. B. KITCHEN DINING 18'x10'-5" OPT'L DOOR

C.

LDR'Y C.

26'-0" HTR. CLO. PLAN 2 GARAGE 19'-8" x 23'-4"

L.

B.

BED ROOM 12'x11' C. LIVING ROOM 17'-8"x14'-6"

MAIN AREA

PRICE CODE A

SMALL YET COMFORTABLE HOME

No. 90146

■ This plan features:

— Three bedrooms

— Two full baths

■ A tiled Foyer area with a convenient coat closet

■ A L-shaped open layout between the Living Room and the Dining Room allowing for entertaining ease

■ An eat-in Kitchen with double sinks and adequate counter and storage area

■ A secluded Master Bedroom that includes a full bath

■ An optional basement or crawl space foundation — please specify when ordering

MAIN AREA— 1,500 SQ. FT.

TOTAL LIVING AREA:
1,500 SQ. FT.

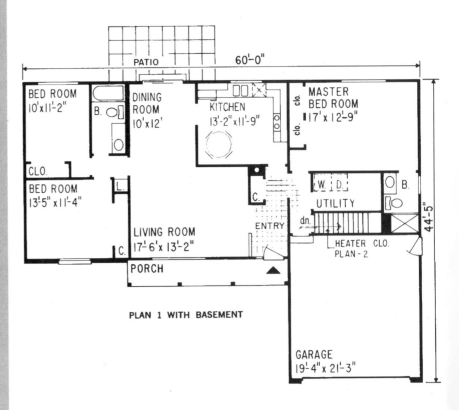

PLAN 1 WITH BASEMENT

PRICE CODE D

DECK DOUBLES OUTDOOR LIVING SPACE

An
EXCLUSIVE DESIGN
By Karl Kreeger

No. 10619

■ This plan features:

— Three bedrooms

— Three baths

■ A design made for the sun lover with a front deck and patio

■ A sunken Living Room with three window walls and a massive fireplace.

■ A hot tub with skylight, a vaulted Master Suite and a utility area

FIRST FLOOR — 2,352 SQ. FT.
BASEMENT — 2,352 SQ. FT.
GARAGE — 696 SQ. FT.

TOTAL LIVING AREA:
2,352 SQ. FT.

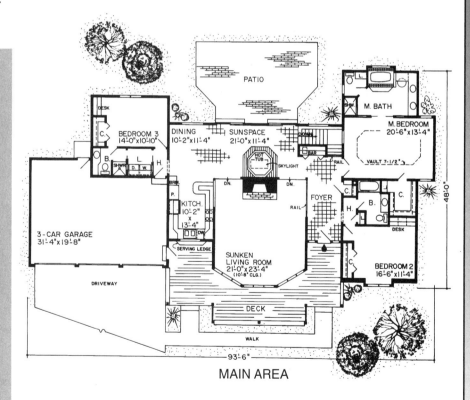

MAIN AREA

PRICE CODE B

AN ENERGY EFFICIENT HOME

No. 90165

- This plan features:
- — Three bedrooms
- — Two full baths
- A step-saving ranch layout with the bedrooms situated on one side of the home
- A U-shaped Kitchen equipped with a peninsula counter/eating bar, double sink, and laundry area
- A Great Room that may include a fireplace, open to the Dining Area enhancing spaciousness
- A roomy Master Bedroom equipped with a walk-in closet and private Bath
- Two additional bedrooms, one as a Den possibility, that share a full hall bath
- This plan is available with a basement foundation only

MAIN AREA — 1,605 SQ. FT.

**TOTAL LIVING AREA:
1,605 SQ. FT.**

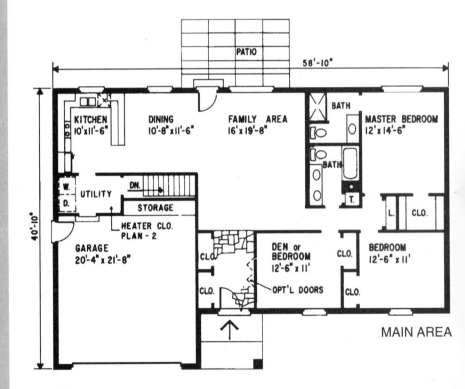

MAIN AREA

PRICE CODE B

YOUR CLASSIC HIDEAWAY

No. 90423

■ This plan features:

— Three bedrooms

— Two full baths

■ A lovely fireplace in the Living Room, which is both cozy and a source of heat for the core area

■ An efficient country Kitchen connecting the large Dining and Living Rooms

■ A lavish Master Suite enhanced by a step-up sunken tub, more than ample closet space, and separate shower

■ A screened porch and patio area for outdoor living

■ An optional basement, slab or crawl space foundation — please specify when ordering

MAIN AREA — 1,773 SQ. FT.
SCREENED PORCH — 240 SQ. FT.

TOTAL LIVING AREA:
1,773 SQ. FT.

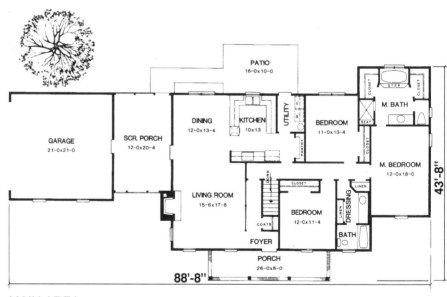

MAIN AREA

PRICE CODE A

COMPACT HOME IS SURPRISINGLY SPACIOUS

An EXCLUSIVE DESIGN
By Westhome Planners, Ltd.

No. 90905

■ This plan features:

— Three bedrooms

— Two full baths

■ A spacious Living Room warmed by a fireplace

■ A Dining Room flowing off the Living Room, with sliding glass doors to the deck

■ An efficient, well-equipped Kitchen with a snack bar, double sink, and ample cabinet and counter space

■ A Master Suite with a walk-in closet and private full bath

■ Two additional, roomy bedrooms with ample closet space and protection from street noise from the two-car garage

MAIN AREA — 1,314 SQ. FT.
BASEMENT — 1,488 SQ. FT.
GARAGE — 484 SQ. FT.
WIDTH — 50'-0"
DEPTH — 54'-0"

TOTAL LIVING AREA:
1,314 SQ. FT.

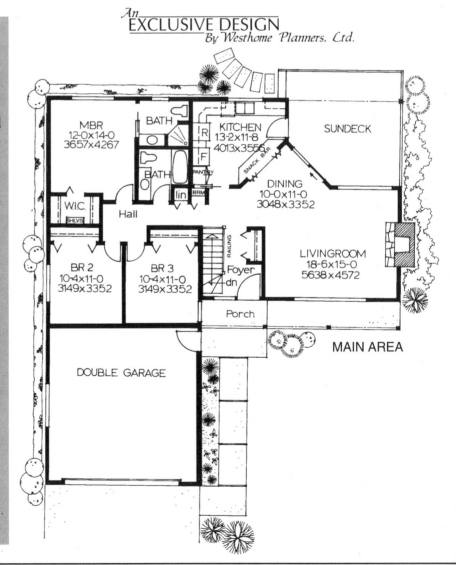

PRICE CODE A

SMALL SCALE, LOTS OF SPACE

No. 90390

■ This plan features:

— Two bedrooms with optional third bedroom/den

— Two full baths

■ Vaulted ceilings and corner windows

■ A Living Room enhanced by a cozy corner fireplace

■ A Master Suite featuring interesting angles and corner window treatments

MAIN AREA — 1,231 SQ. FT.

TOTAL LIVING AREA: 1,231 SQ. FT.

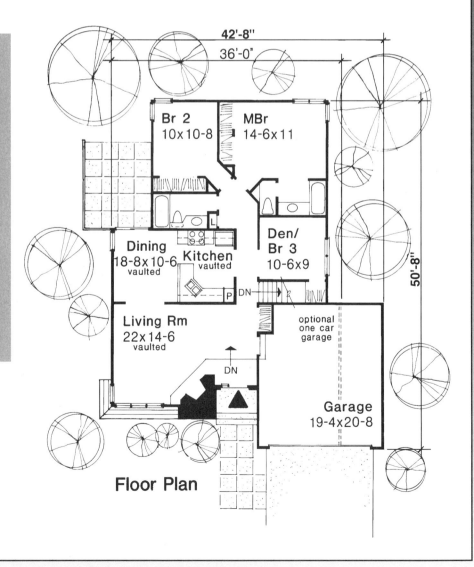

Floor Plan

PRICE CODE B

CAREFREE ONE-LEVEL CONVENIENCE

No. 10674

■ This plan features:

— Three bedrooms

— Two full baths

■ A galley Kitchen, centrally-located between the Dining, Breakfast and Living Room areas

■ A huge Family Room which exits onto the patio

■ The Master Suite with double closets and vanities

MAIN AREA — 1,600 SQ. FT.
GARAGE — 465 SQ. FT.

**TOTAL LIVING AREA:
1,600 SQ. FT.**

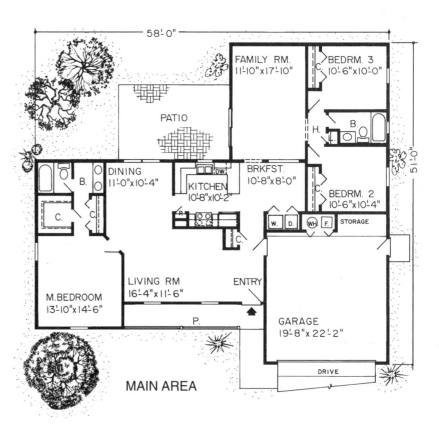

MAIN AREA

PRICE CODE A

FAMILY FAVORITE

No. 20156

■ This plan features:

— Three bedrooms

— Two full baths

■ An open arrangement with the Dining Room that combines with ten foot ceilings to make the Living Room seem more spacious

■ Glass on three sides of the Dining Room which overlooks the deck

■ An efficient, compact Kitchen with a built-in pantry and peninsula counter

■ A Master Suite with a romantic window seat, a compartmentalized private bath and a walk-in closet

■ Two additional bedrooms that share a full hall closet

FIRST FLOOR — 1,359 SQ. FT.
BASEMENT — 1,359 SQ. FT.
GARAGE — 501 SQ. FT.

**TOTAL LIVING AREA:
1,359 SQ. FT.**

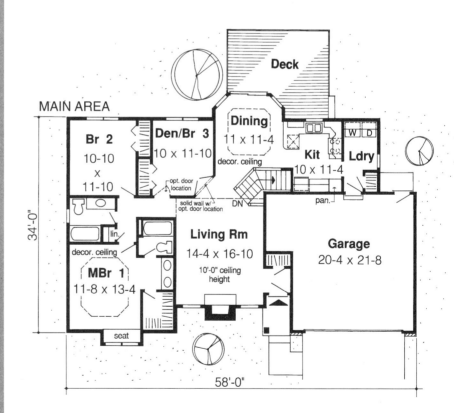

An
EXCLUSIVE DESIGN
By Karl Kreeger

PRICE CODE B

CONVENIENT SINGLE LEVEL

No. 84056

■ This plan features:

— Three bedrooms

— Two full baths

■ A well-appointed U-shaped Kitchen that includes a view of the front yard and a built-in pantry

■ An expansive Great Room with direct access to the rear yard, expanding the living space

■ A Master Bedroom equipped with two closets—one is a walk-in— and a private bath

■ Two additional bedrooms that share a full hall bath

■ A step-saving, centrally located laundry center

FIRST FLOOR — 1,644 SQ. FT.
GARAGE — 576 SQ. FT.

TOTAL LIVING AREA:
1,644 SQ. FT.

No materials list available

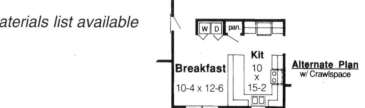

PRICE CODE B

COMPACT PLAN ALLOWS FOR GRACIOUS LIVING

No. 90158

■ This plan features:

— Three bedrooms

— Two full baths

■ A Great Room, accessible from the Foyer, offering cathedral ceilings, exposed beams, and a brick fireplace

■ A Kitchen with a center island and cathedral ceiling, accented by a round-top window

■ A Master Bedroom with a full bath and a walk-in closet

■ An optional basement, slab or crawl space foundation — please specify when ordering

MAIN AREA — 1,540 SQ. FT.
BASEMENT — 1,540 SQ. FT.

TOTAL LIVING AREA:
1,540 SQ. FT.

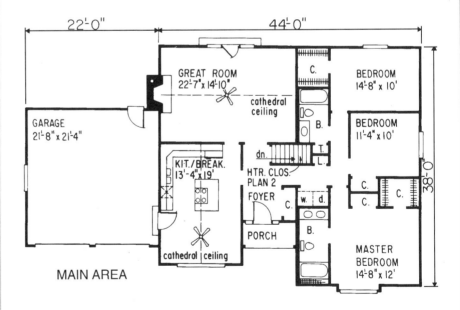

MAIN AREA

PRICE CODE B

VARIED ROOF HEIGHTS CREATE INTERESTING LINES

No. 90601

■ This plan features:

— Three bedrooms

— Two full baths

■ A spacious Family Room with a heat-circulating fireplace, which is visible from the Foyer

■ A large Kitchen with a cooktop island, opening into the dinette bay

■ A Master Suite with his-n-her closets and a private Master Bath

■ Two additional bedrooms which share a full hall bath

■ Formal Dining and Living Rooms, flowing into each other for easy entertaining

MAIN AREA — 1,613 SQ. FT.

TOTAL LIVING AREA:
1,613 SQ. FT.

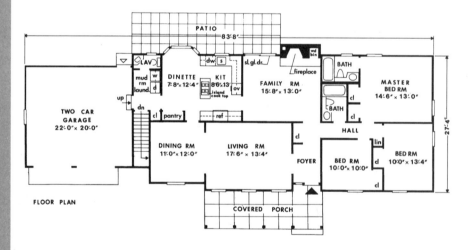

FLOOR PLAN

PRICE CODE A

HIGH IMPACT ANGLES

No. 90357

- This plan features:
- — Three bedrooms
- — Two full baths
- Soaring ceilings to give the house a spacious, contemporary feeling
- A fireplaced Great Room adjoining a convenient Kitchen, with a sunny Breakfast Nook
- Sliding glass doors opening onto an angular deck
- A Master Suite with vaulted ceilings and a private bath

MAIN AREA — 1,368 SQ. FT.

TOTAL LIVING AREA:
1,368 SQ. FT.

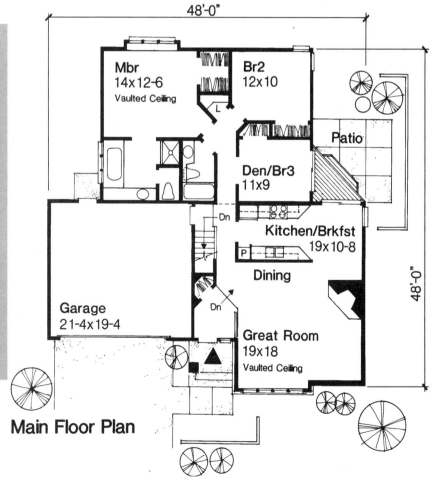

Main Floor Plan

PRICE CODE B

CONVENIENT CLASSIC WITH MODERN UPDATES

No. 20110

■ This plan features:

— Three bedrooms

— Two full baths

■ Clapboard and brick lending curbside appeal

■ A spacious Living Room dominated by a corner fireplace

■ A hallway off the foyer, leading to the two additional bedrooms

■ A formal Dining Room and a sky-lit Breakfast Nook adjoining the Kitchen

■ A rear deck perfect for summer barbecues or relaxing

■ A Master Suite with a double vanity, a raised bath and a walk-in shower

MAIN AREA — 1,786 SQ. FT.
BASEMENT — 1,786 SQ. FT.
GARAGE — 484 SQ. FT.

TOTAL LIVING AREA:
1,786 SQ. FT.

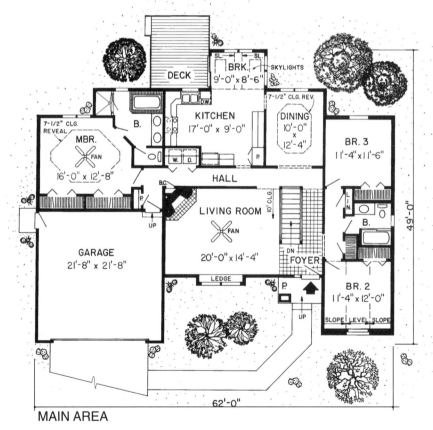

MAIN AREA

An
EXCLUSIVE DESIGN
By Karl Kreeger

PRICE CODE B

WINDOWS ADD WARMTH TO ALL LIVING AREAS

No. 34011

■ This plan features:

— Three bedrooms

— Two full baths

■ A Master Suite with huge his-n-her walk-in closets and private bath

■ A second and third bedroom with ample closet space

■ A Kitchen equipped with an island counter, and flowing easily into the Dining and Family Rooms

■ A Laundry Room conveniently located near all three bedrooms

■ An optional garage

MAIN AREA — 1,672 SQ. FT.
OPTIONAL GARAGE — 566 SQ. FT.

TOTAL LIVING AREA:
1,672 SQ. FT.

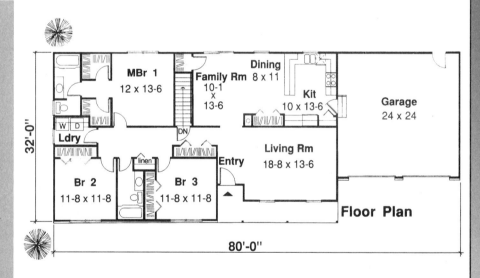

Floor Plan

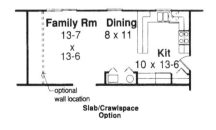

Slab/Crawlspace Option

PRICE CODE C

RANCH OFFERS ATTRACTIVE WINDOW FACADE

No. 10569

■ This plan features:

— Four bedrooms

— Three full baths

■ A Living Room with sloping, open-beamed ceilings and a fireplace with built-in bookshelves

■ A Dining Room with a vaulted ceiling, adding a feeling of spaciousness

■ A Master Bath with ample closet space and a private bath

■ A two-car garage

FIRST FLOOR — 1,840 SQ. FT.
BASEMENT — 1,803 SQ. FT.
GARAGE — 445 SQ. FT.

**TOTAL LIVING AREA:
1,840 SQ. FT.**

An
EXCLUSIVE DESIGN
By Karl Kreeger

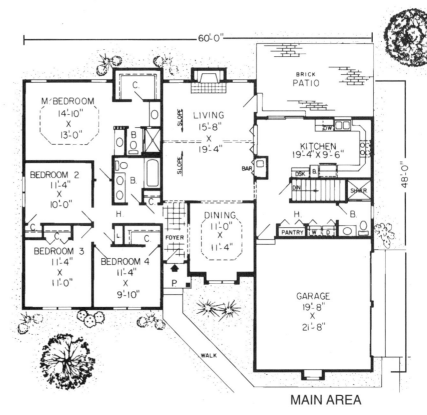

MAIN AREA

PRICE CODE A

GREAT ROOM FEATURES FIREPLACE

No. 90105

■ This plan features:

— Three bedrooms

— Two full baths

■ A spacious Great Room with a cozy fireplace

■ A Kitchen with a pass through serving for convenience

■ A combination Mud Room/Laundry Room to make cleaning up a breeze

■ An optional basement, slab or crawl space foundation — please specify when ordering

MAIN AREA — 1,345 SQ. FT.

TOTAL LIVING AREA:
1,345 SQ. FT.

MAIN AREA

PRICE CODE A

SLOPED CEILINGS ENHANCE OPEN FLOOR PLAN

No. 90125

■ This plan features:

— Three bedrooms

— Two full baths

■ A step down into the tiled entrance area

■ An open Great Room and Living Room enhanced by sloping ceilings, cozy fireplace, and sliding doors to back patio

■ An L shaped Kitchen sharing snack bar with Dining Room

■ An optional basement or crawlspace foundation — please specify when ordering

MAIN AREA — 1,440 SQ. FT.

**TOTAL LIVING AREA:
1,440 SQ. FT.**

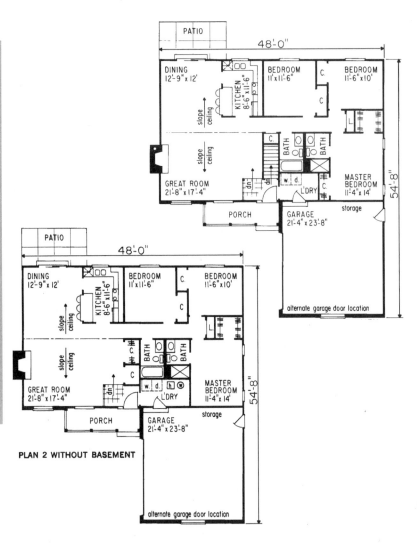

PLAN 2 WITHOUT BASEMENT

PRICE CODE A

EXTRA LARGE FAMILY KITCHEN IN COZY THREE BEDROOM

No. 90134

■ This plan features:

— Three bedrooms

— One full and one half baths

■ A sheltered porch providing a protected entrance

■ An extra large Kitchen, with a galley-style food preparation area, separated from the rest of the room by an eating bar

■ Three bedrooms clustered around the full bath

■ A large outdoor storage area built into the back of the carport

■ An optional basement, slab or crawl space foundation — please specify when ordering

MAIN AREA — 1,120 SQ. FT.

TOTAL LIVING AREA:
1,120 SQ. FT.

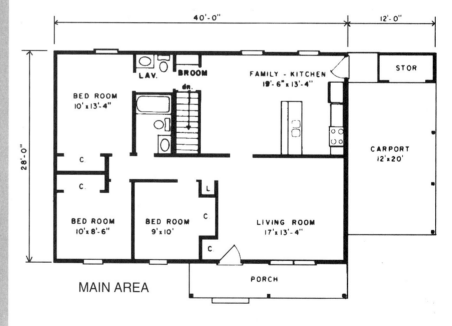

MAIN AREA

PRICE CODE B

ROOMY RANCH WITH CONTEMPORARY FLAIR

No. 10594

■ This plan features:

— Two bedrooms with optional third bedroom

— Two full baths

■ A sloping, open-beamed ceiling and a wood-burning fireplace in the Great Room

■ A Dining Room with sliding glass doors leading onto a large wooden deck

■ A laundry room near the Kitchen and Dining Room

MAIN AREA — 1,565 SQ. FT.
BASEMENT — 1,576 SQ. FT.
GARAGE — 430 SQ. FT.

TOTAL LIVING AREA:
1,565 SQ. FT.

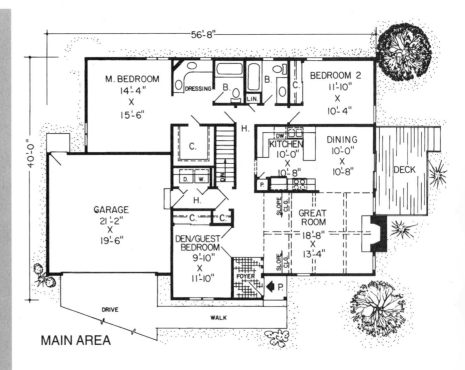

MAIN AREA

An
EXCLUSIVE DESIGN
By Karl Kreeger

SUNBELT HOMES

PRICE CODE B

No. 20116

■ This plan features:

— Three bedrooms

— Two full baths

■ Slender columns and brick detailing lending a Georgian flavor to the facade

■ An entry that opens upon a formal Living Room, equipped with a focal point fireplace, elegant arched windows, and high ceilings

■ A bay window enhancing the formal Dining Room

■ A U-shaped Kitchen with a double sink and ample work space

■ A tray ceiling, crowning a lovely and private Master Suite, enhanced by a double vanitied Bath and a walk-in closet

■ Two additional bedrooms, with walk-in closets, convenient to the full hall bath

MAIN AREA — 1,677 SQ. FT.
BASEMENT — 1,653 SQ. FT.
GARAGE — 520 SQ. FT.

TOTAL LIVING AREA:
1,677 SQ. FT.

GEORGIAN GRACE

An
EXCLUSIVE DESIGN
By Karl Kreeger

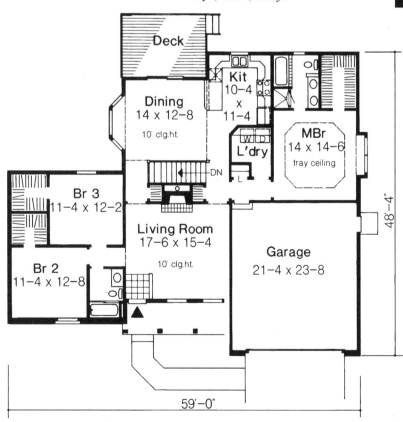

PRICE CODE B

PLANNED FOR A VIEW

No. 90979

■ This plan features:

— Three bedrooms

— Two full baths

■ A comfortable, stucco ranch with a covered entrance leading into a open Living/Dining Room area with an unusual corner window treatment

■ A U-shaped Kitchen offering a built-in pantry, a bright, eating Nook and a snackbar adjoining the Family Room

■ A spacious Family Room with a tiled fireplace and sliding glass doors to a large, partially covered Sundeck

■ A Master Bedroom, accented by an arched window and a vaulted ceiling, with a walk-in closet and a private bath

MAIN FLOOR — 1,597 SQ. FT.
BASEMENT — 1,590 SQ. FT.
WIDTH — 46'-0"
DEPTH — 54'-0"

TOTAL LIVING AREA:
1,597 SQ. FT.

No materials list available

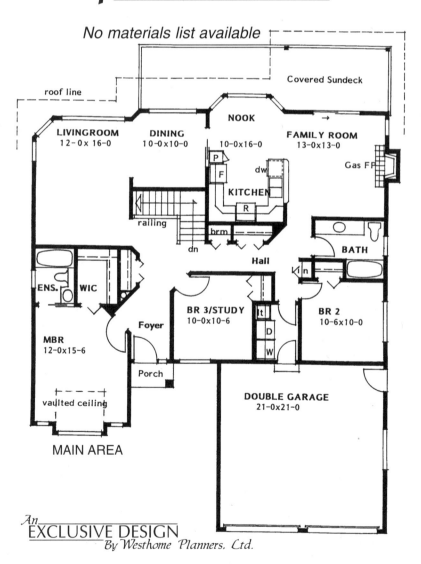

An
EXCLUSIVE DESIGN
By Westhome Planners, Ltd.

PRICE CODE B

No. 90986

■ This plan features:

— Three bedrooms

— Two full baths

■ An Italian style, featuring columns and tile originally designed to sit on the edge of a golf course

■ An open design with panoramic vistas in every direction

■ Tile used from the Foyer, into the Kitchen and Nook, as well as in the Utility Room

■ A whirlpool tub in the elaborate and spacious Master Bedroom suite

■ A Great Room with a corner gas fireplace

■ A turreted Breakfast Nook and an efficient Kitchen with peninsula counter

■ Two family bedrooms that share a full hall bath

MAIN AREA — 1,731 SQ. FT.
GARAGE — 888 SQ. FT.
WIDTH — 74'-0"
DEPTH — 45'-0"

TOTAL LIVING AREA:
1,731 SQ. FT.

SURROUNDED WITH SUNSHINE

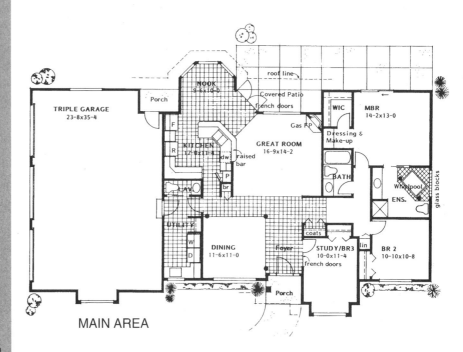

MAIN AREA

An
EXCLUSIVE DESIGN
By Westhome Planners, Ltd.

PRICE CODE D

MORNING ROOM ACCENTS

No. 10445

■ This plan features:

— Three bedrooms

— Two and one half baths

■ Tiled floors unifying the Dining and food preparation areas

■ A Morning Room located off the well-organized Kitchen

■ A Family Room employing more tile accents which opens to the patio

■ A secluded Master Bedroom which includes a sunken tub, small greenhouses, and ample closet space

FIRST FLOOR — 2,466 SQ. FT.
GARAGE — 482 SQ. FT.

TOTAL LIVING AREA:
2,466 SQ. FT.

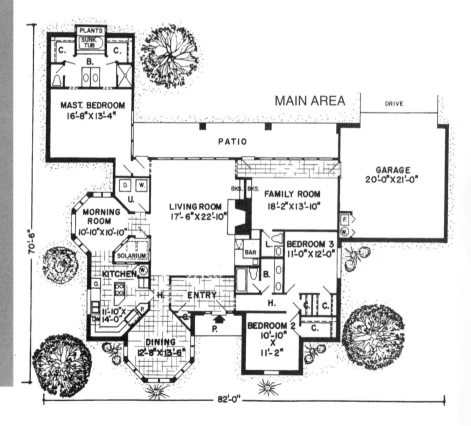

PRICE CODE A

FEATURES FOUND IN LARGE HOMES

No. 10509

■ This plan features:

— Three bedrooms

— Two full baths

■ A tiled Entry leading into a spacious Living Room

■ A Living Room/Dining area featuring a fireplace with an extended hearth flanked by glass windows and sliding doors

■ An efficient Kitchen with plenty of counter space and a food bar adjacent to the Living Room

■ An inviting Master Suite with a dressing area, a walk-in closet and a private bath

■ Two additional bedrooms, one with a built-in dressing table, sharing a full hall bath

MAIN FLOOR — 1,464 SQ. FT.
GARAGE — 528 SQ. FT.

TOTAL LIVING AREA:
1,464 SQ. FT.

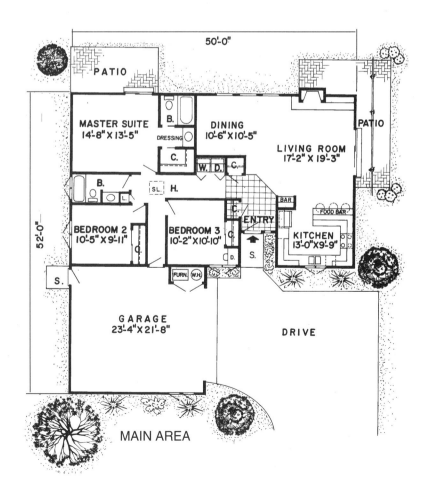

MAIN AREA

PRICE CODE A

FORMAL BALANCE

No. 90689

■ This plan features:

— Three bedrooms

— Two full baths

■ A cathedral ceiling in the Living Room with a heat-circulating fireplace as the focal point

■ A bow window in the Dining Room that adds elegance as well as natural light

■ A well-equipped Kitchen that serves both the Dinette and the formal Dining Room efficiently

■ A Master Bedroom with three closets and a private Master Bath with sliding glass doors to the Master Deck with a hot tub

FIRST FLOOR — 1,374 SQ. FT.
MUDROOM/LAUNDRY — 102 SQ. FT.
BASEMENT — 1,361 SQ. FT.
GARAGE — 548 SQ. FT.

TOTAL LIVING AREA:
1,476 SQ. FT.

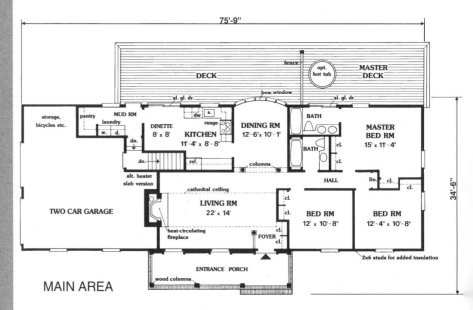

MAIN AREA

PRICE CODE F

A CELEBRATION OF TRADITIONAL ELEMENTS

No. 10749

■ This plan features:

— Four bedrooms

— Two full and two half baths

■ High ceilings with cooling fans and loads of built-in storage

■ Every bedroom adjoining a bath and the Master Suite enjoying access to the outdoor deck

■ A massive fireplace located the roomy Family Room

■ A Kitchen, Breakfast area, Sewing room, Dining Room and pantry all located within steps of each other for convenience

FIRST FLOOR — 3,438 SQ. FT.
GARAGE — 610 SQ. FT.

TOTAL LIVING AREA:
3,438 SQ. FT.

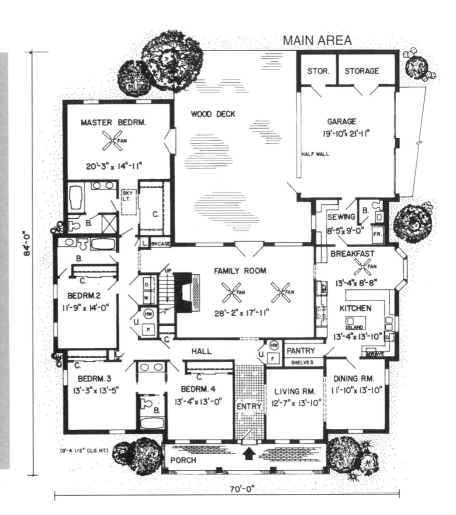

PRICE CODE E

SUPERIOR COMFORT AND PRIVACY

No. 9828

■ This plan features:

— Four bedrooms

— Three full baths

■ A natural stone exterior with slate floors in the Foyer and leading to the private patio off the Master Bedroom

■ A two-way fireplace between the Living Room and Family Room

■ A Breakfast Nook with a large bow window facing the terrace and pool

■ Four bedrooms grouped in one wing for privacy

FIRST FLOOR — 2,679 SQ. FT.
BASEMENT — 2,679 SQ. FT.
GARAGE — 541 SQ. FT.

TOTAL LIVING AREA:
2,679 SQ. FT.

PRICE CODE B

INSPIRED BY COUNTRY PORCHES OF OLD

No. 20211

■ This plan features:
— Three bedrooms
— Two full baths

■ Decorative and sloped ceilings

■ A large country Kitchen with a central island, double sink, pantry, ample cabinet and counter space and access to deck

■ A Master Suite with a decorative ceiling, walk-in closet and a private Master Bath

■ A decorative Dining Room ceiling

■ A central fireplace in the sloped ceilinged Living Room, providing a focal point and adding warmth to the room

■ Two additional bedrooms that share use of a full hall bath

MAIN AREA — 1,609 SQ. FT.
GARAGE — 707 SQ. FT.
BASEMENT — 902 SQ. FT.

TOTAL LIVING AREA:
1,609 SQ. FT.

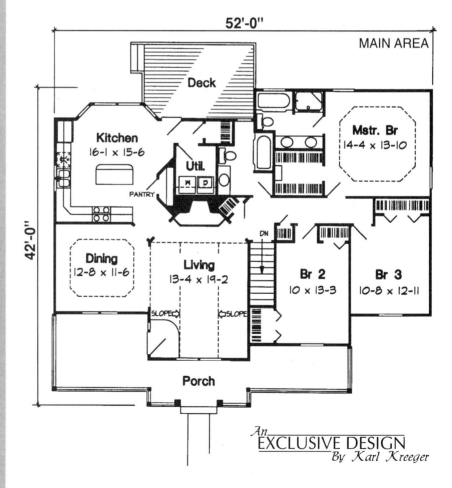

An
EXCLUSIVE DESIGN
By Karl Kreeger

PRICE CODE B

CAREFREE COMFORT

No. 91418

■ This plan features:

— Three bedrooms

— Two full baths

■ A dramatic vaulted Foyer

■ A range top island Kitchen with a sunny eating Nook surrounded by a built-in planter

■ A vaulted ceiling in the Great Room with a built-in bar and corner fireplace

■ A bayed Dining Room that combines with the Great Room for a spacious feeling

■ A Master Bedroom with a private reading nook, vaulted ceiling, walk-in closet, and a well-appointed private Bath

■ Two additional bedrooms sharing a full hall bath

MAIN AREA — 1,665 SQ. FT.
GARAGE — 2-CAR

TOTAL LIVING AREA:
1,665 SQ. FT.

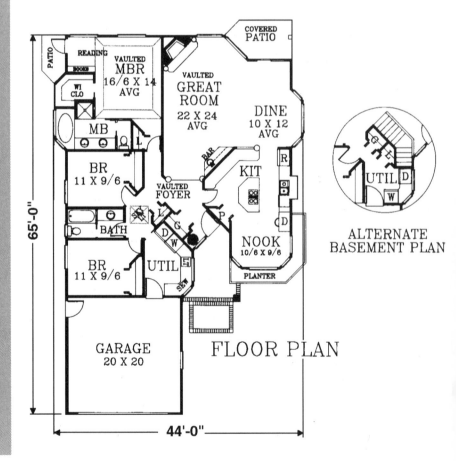

FLOOR PLAN

ALTERNATE
BASEMENT PLAN

PRICE CODE B

DAYTIME DELIGHT

No. 91607

■ This plan features:

— Three bedrooms

— Two full baths

■ A large, vaulted ceiling in the Living Room and Dining Room, that flows together and is accentuated by huge windows

■ A centrally-located Kitchen with a double sink, and ample cabinet and counter space

■ A glass-walled eating Nook with access to a covered porch

■ A vaulted ceiling in the Family Room, with a focal point fireplace

■ An exciting Master Suite with a vaulted ceiling, a walk-in closet and a private double-vanity bath

■ Two additional bedrooms, one with French doors, served by a full hall bath

MAIN AREA — 1,653 SQ. FT.

TOTAL LIVING AREA:
1,653 SQ. FT.

An
EXCLUSIVE DESIGN
By Mark Stewart

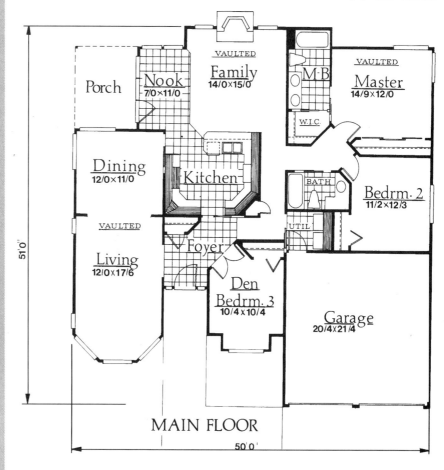

MAIN FLOOR

PRICE CODE A

INVITING PORCH ADORNS AFFORDABLE HOME

No. 90682

■ This plan features:

— Three bedrooms

— Two full baths

■ A large and spacious Living Room that adjoins the Dining Room for ease in entertaining

■ A private bedroom wing offering a quiet atmosphere

■ A Master Bedroom with his-n-her closets and a private bath

■ An efficient Kitchen with a walk-in pantry

MAIN AREA — 1,160 SQ. FT.
LAUNDRY/MUDROOM — 83 SQ. FT.

TOTAL LIVING AREA:
1,243 SQ. FT.

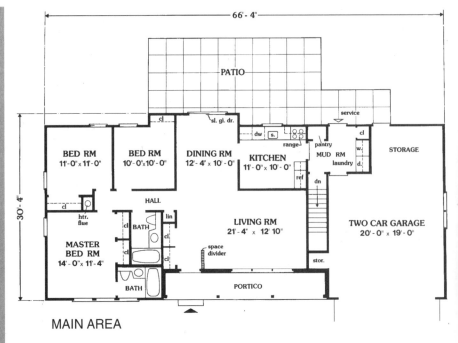

MAIN AREA

PRICE CODE B

CAREFREE CONTEMPORARY

No. 90697

■ This plan features:

— Three bedrooms

— Two full baths

■ A corner fireplace adding intrigue to the sunny Living Room

■ Skylights in the high sloping ceiling of the Family Room, which also has a greenhouse bay window and a heat-circulating fireplace

■ An elegant formal Dining Room with a window alcove

■ A Master Bedroom with a private Master Bath and two closets

■ Two additional bedrooms which share a full hall bath

MAIN AREA — 1,597 SQ. FT.
BASEMENT — 1,512 SQ. FT.

TOTAL LIVING AREA:
1,597 SQ. FT.

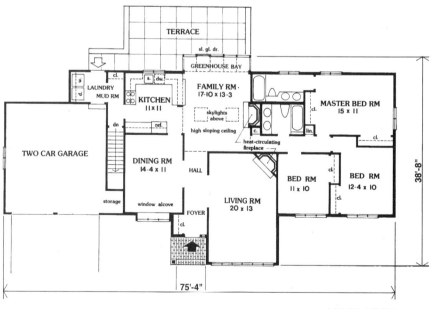

MAIN AREA

PRICE CODE D

*I*NDOOR AND OUTDOOR LIVING

No. 26952

■ This plan features:

— Three bedrooms

— Three full baths

■ An Entry Deck leading into the Foyer and the Great Room with a cathedral ceiling, and over-sized hearth fireplace

■ French doors galore in the Master Bedroom, the Great Room, the Kitchen, to the expansive Deck, the Swimming Pool, the Sauna and the Pool Bath

■ A Kitchen with a built-in pantry and a desk, cooktop island adjacent to the Utility Room and the Garage

■ A Master Bedroom suite with a cathedral ceiling, plush Master bath with a walk-in closet, and access to the two decks

■ Two additional bedrooms with over-sized closets, sharing a deck and full hall bath

MAIN FLOOR — 2,484 SQ. FT.
SAUNA & POOL BATH — 84 SQ. FT.
GARAGE — 418 SQ. FT.

TOTAL LIVING AREA:
2,568 SQ. FT.

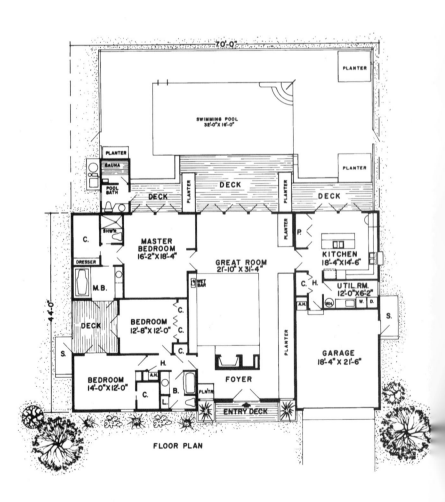

FLOOR PLAN

PRICE CODE C

DRAMATIC IMPRESSIONS

No. 20451

■ This plan features:

— Three bedrooms

— Two full and one half baths

■ A soaring Living Room off the vaulted, sky-lit Foyer

■ A cozy Family Room that shares the backyard view with the glass-walled Breakfast room

■ A Kitchen that easily serves every area, including the elegant, formal Dining Room at the front of the house

■ A Master Suite, tucked behind the garage, including private deck access, and a magnificent Bath with a garden tub

FIRST FLOOR — 2,084 SQ. FT.

TOTAL LIVING AREA:
2,084 SQ. FT.

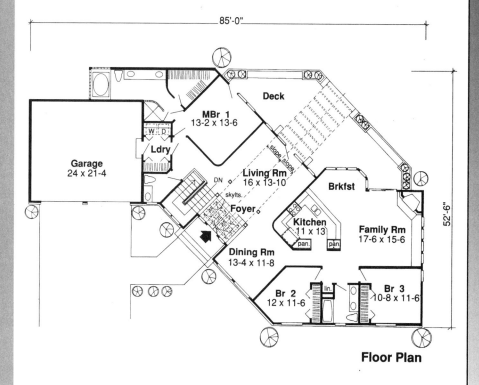

Floor Plan

PRICE CODE B

COMFORT AND CONVENIENCE

No. 93402

■ This plan features:

— Three bedrooms

— Two full baths

■ Ranch styled one floor living

■ An island Kitchen/Breakfast area that is spacious and includes ample cabinet and counter space

■ A Family Room with a fireplace and direct access to the patio and porch

■ An elegant formal Dining Room that is convenient to the Kitchen

■ A Master Suite with a walk-in closet and private Master Bath

■ Two additional bedrooms that share a full hall bath

MAIN AREA — 1,739 SQ. FT.

GARAGE — 509 SQ. FT.

TOTAL LIVING AREA: 1,739 SQ. FT.

No materials list available

An
EXCLUSIVE DESIGN
By Greg Marquis

PRICE CODE C

COZY TRADITIONAL

No. 93000

■ This plan features:
— Three bedrooms
— Two full baths

■ An angled eating bar separating the Kitchen, Breakfast Room and Great Room, while leaving these areas open for easy entertaining

■ An efficient, well-appointed Kitchen that is convenient to both the formal Dining Room and the sunny Breakfast Room

■ A spacious Master Suite with oval tub, step-in shower, double vanity and walk-in closet

■ Two additional bedrooms with ample closet space that share a full hall bath

FIRST FLOOR — 1,862 SQ. FT.
GARAGE — 520 SQ. FT.

TOTAL LIVING AREA:
1,862 SQ. FT.

No materials list available

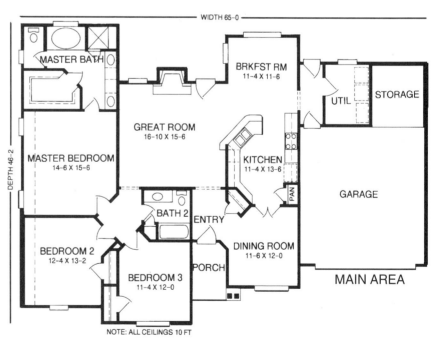

WIDTH 65-0

DEPTH 46-2

MASTER BATH

MASTER BEDROOM
14-6 X 15-6

GREAT ROOM
16-10 X 15-6

BRKFST RM
11-4 X 11-6

UTIL

STORAGE

KITCHEN
11-4 X 13-6

PAN

GARAGE

BATH 2

ENTRY

BEDROOM 2
12-4 X 13-2

BEDROOM 3
11-4 X 12-0

PORCH

DINING ROOM
11-6 X 12-0

MAIN AREA

NOTE: ALL CEILINGS 10 FT

An
EXCLUSIVE DESIGN
By Belk Home Designs

PRICE CODE B

FOR THE DISCRIMINATING BUYER

No. 92625

■ This plan features:

— Three bedrooms

— Two full baths

■ An attractive, classic brick design, with wood trim, multiple gables, and wing walls

■ A sheltered entrance into the Foyer

■ A sloped ceiling adding elegance to the formal Dining Room

■ A sloped ceiling and a corner fireplace enhancing the Great Room

■ A peninsula counter in the Kitchen and the Breakfast Room

■ A Master Suite equipped with a large walk-in closet and a private bath with an oval corner tub, separate shower and double vanity

■ Two additional bedrooms

MAIN AREA — 1,710 SQ. FT.
BASEMENT — 1,560 SQ. FT.
GARAGE — 455 SQ. FT.
WIDTH — 65'-10"
DEPTH — 56'-0"

TOTAL LIVING AREA:
1,710 SQ. FT.

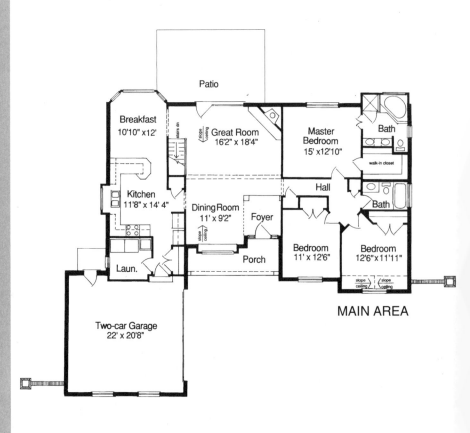

MAIN AREA

No materials list available

PRICE CODE C

PLUSH MASTER BEDROOM WING

No. 92705

■ This plan features:

— Three bedrooms

— Two full baths

■ A raised, tile Foyer with a decorative window leading into an expansive Living Room, accented by a tiled fireplace and framed by French doors

■ An efficient Kitchen with a walk-in pantry and serving bar adjoining the Breakfast and Utility areas

■ A private Master Bedroom, crowned by a stepped ceiling, offering an atrium door to outside, a huge, walk-in closet and a luxurious bath

MAIN FLOOR — 1,849 SQ. FT.
GARAGE — 437 SQ. FT.

TOTAL LIVING AREA:
1,849 SQ. FT.

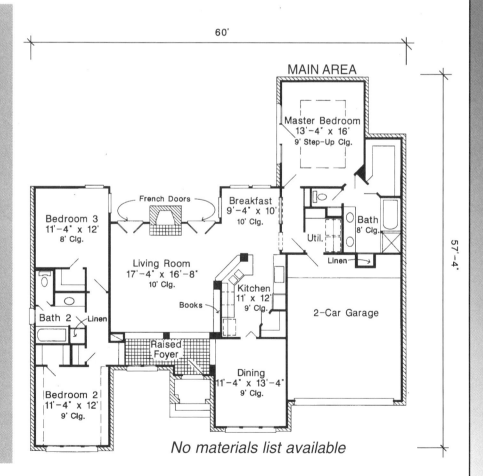

No materials list available

PRICE CODE C

CHARMING BRICK HOME

No. 93107

■ This plan features:

— Three bedrooms

— Two full baths

■ A covered entrance leading into a spacious Living Room with a fireplace and an airy Dining Room with access to the Patio

■ An island Kitchen, open to the Dining Room, offering ample storage and easy access to the Laundry area and the Garage

■ A Master Bedroom with a walk-in closet, access to the Patio and a plush bath offering a window tub, a step-in shower and a double vanity

■ Two additional bedrooms, with decorative windows, sharing a full hall bath

MAIN FLOOR — 1,868 SQ. FT.
BASEMENT — 1,868 SQ. FT.

TOTAL LIVING AREA:
1,868 SQ. FT.

No materials list available

WIDTH 72'-0"
DEPTH 42'-4"

MAIN FLOOR

An
EXCLUSIVE DESIGN
By Ahmann Design Inc.

PRICE CODE B

STYLISH SINGLE-LEVEL

No. 93100

■ This plan features:

— Three bedrooms

— Two full and one half baths

■ A well-appointed, U-shaped Kitchen separated from the Dining Room by a peninsula counter

■ A spacious Living Room, enhanced by a focal point fireplace

■ An elegant Dining Room with a bay window that opens to a screen porch, expanding living space

■ A Master Suite with a walk-in closet and private Master Bath

■ Two family bedrooms that share a full hall bath

MAIN AREA — 1,642 SQ. FT.
GARAGE — 591 SQ. FT.
BASEMENT — 1,642 SQ. FT.

TOTAL LIVING AREA:
1,642 SQ. FT.

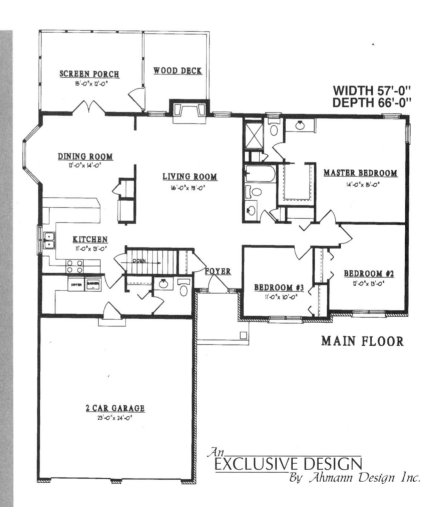

WIDTH 57'-0"
DEPTH 66'-0"

MAIN FLOOR

An EXCLUSIVE DESIGN
By Ahmann Design Inc.

PRICE CODE A

SPECTACULAR TRADITIONAL

No. 92502

■ This plan features:

— Three bedrooms

— Two full baths

■ The use of gable roofs and the blend of stucco and brick to form a spectacular exterior

■ A high vaulted ceiling and a cozy fireplace, with built-in cabinets in the Den

■ An efficient, U-shaped Kitchen with an adjacent Dining Area

■ A Master Bedroom, with a raised ceiling, that includes a private bath and a walk-in closet

■ Two family bedrooms that share a full hall bath

MAIN AREA — 1,237 SQ. FT.
GARAGE — 436 SQ. FT.

TOTAL LIVING AREA:
1,237 SQ. FT.

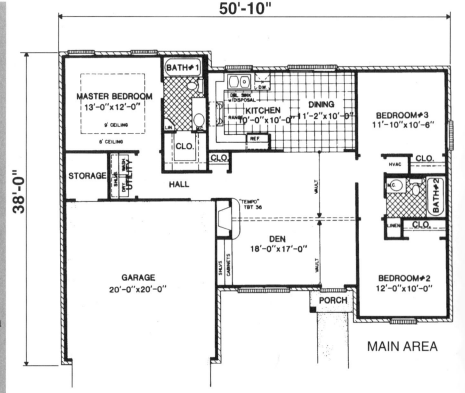

MAIN AREA

PRICE CODE A

AMENITY PACKED WITH AFFORDABILITY

No. 92525

■ This plan features:

— Three bedrooms

— Two full baths

■ A sheltered entrance inviting your guests onward

■ A fireplace in the Den offering a focal point, while the decorative ceiling adds definition to the room

■ A well-equipped Kitchen flowing with ease into the Breakfast bay or Dining Room

■ A Master Bedroom, having two closets and a private Master Bath

MAIN AREA — 1,484 SQ. FT.

TOTAL LIVING AREA:
1,484 SQ. FT.

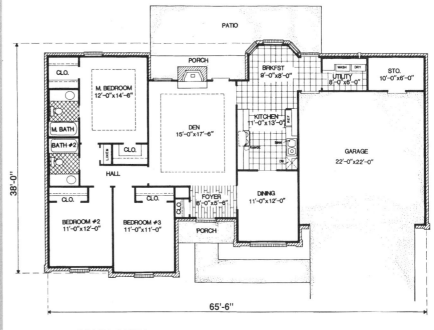

MAIN AREA

PRICE CODE C

FOR THE EMPTY-NESTER

No. 98316

■ This plan features:

— Two bedrooms

— Two full baths

■ A Great Room with a 13′ ceiling and access to the Lanai

■ An island Kitchen with a built-in pantry, desk, and an open layout to the Breakfast area

■ A Master Suite with his and her walk-in closets and a private Master Bath

■ A Den that can function as a third bedroom

FIRST FLOOR — 1,859 SQ. FT.
GARAGE — 393 SQ. FT.

TOTAL LIVING AREA:
1,859 SQ. FT.

Floor Plan

No materials list available

PRICE CODE C

CONVENIENT AND EFFICIENT RANCH

No. 93311

■ This plan features:

— Three bedrooms

— Two full and one half baths

■ A barrel vault ceiling in the Foyer

■ A stepped ceiling in both the Dinette and the formal Dining Room

■ An expansive Gathering Room with a large focal point fireplace and access to the wood deck

■ An efficient Kitchen that includes a work island and a built-in pantry

■ A luxurious Master Suite with a private bath that includes a separate tub and step-in shower

■ Two additional bedrooms that share a full hall bath

FIRST FLOOR — 1,810 SQ. FT.
GARAGE — 528 SQ. FT.

TOTAL LIVING AREA:
1,810 SQ. FT.

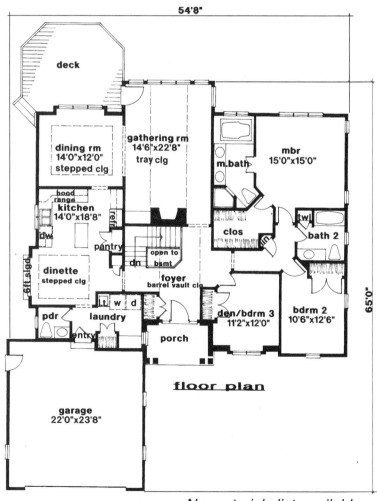

floor plan

An
EXCLUSIVE DESIGN
By Plan One Homes, Inc.

No materials list available

PRICE CODE C

No. 90421

■ This plan features:

— Three bedrooms

— Two full baths

■ A lovely French Provincial design

■ A large Family Room with a raised hearth fireplace and double doors to the patio

■ An L-shaped, island Kitchen with a Breakfast Bay and open counter to the Family Room

■ A Master Suite including one double closet and a compartmentalized bath with walk-in closet, step-up garden tub, double vanity and linen closet

■ Two front bedrooms sharing a full hall bath with a linen closet

■ An optional basement, slab or crawl space foundation — please specify when ordering

FIRST FLOOR — 1,940 SQ. FT.

TOTAL LIVING AREA:
1,940 SQ. FT.

*I*DEAL FOR FORMAL ENTERTAINING

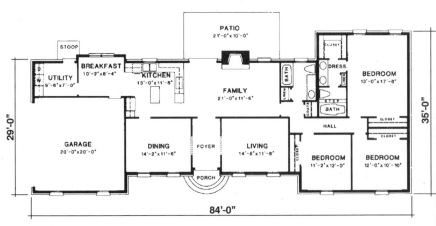

MAIN AREA

PRICE CODE B

CLASSIC FEATURES

No. 90691

- This plan features:
— Three bedrooms
— Two full baths

- A cathedral ceiling in the Living Room with a heat-circulating fireplace

- A spectacular bow window and skylight in the Dining Room

- A sliding glass door and skylight in the Kitchen

- A Master Bedroom including a private Master Bath with a whirlpool tub

- Two additional bedrooms that share a full, double-vanity hall bath

MAIN AREA — 1,530 SQ. FT.
BASEMENT — 1,434 SQ. FT.

TOTAL LIVING AREA:
1,530 SQ. FT.

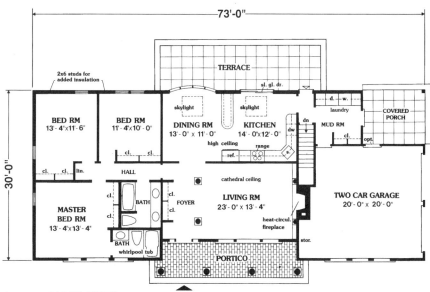

MAIN AREA

PRICE CODE C

ULTIMATE MASTER SUITE

No materials list available

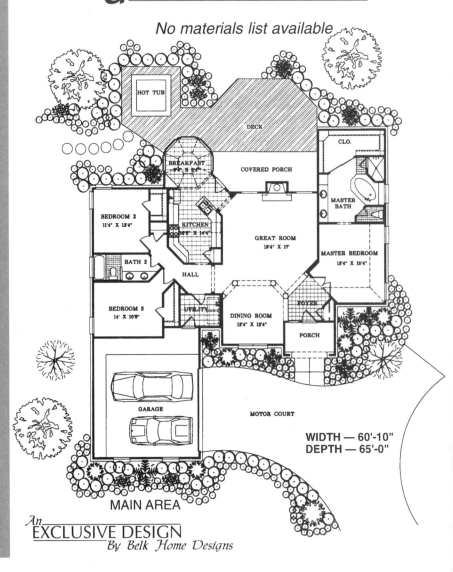

WIDTH — 60'-10"
DEPTH — 65'-0"

MAIN AREA

An
EXCLUSIVE DESIGN
By Belk Home Designs

No. 93030

■ This plan features:

— Three bedrooms

— Two full baths

■ A covered porch leading into the tiled Foyer, a columned Dining Room and an expansive Great Room

■ A large hearth fireplace between sliding glass doors to a covered Porch and a Deck with hot tub

■ A spacious Kitchen with a built-in pantry, a peninsula sink and an octagon-shaped Breakfast area

■ A Master Bedroom wing with French doors, a vaulted ceiling, a plush Master Bath with a huge walk-in closet, a double vanity and a window tub

■ Two additional bedrooms with walk-in closets, sharing a full hall bath

FIRST FLOOR — 1,995 SQ. FT.
GARAGE — 561 SQ. FT.

TOTAL LIVING AREA:
1,995 SQ. FT.

PRICE CODE C

A LONG WRAP-AROUND PORCH

No. 99765

■ This plan features:

— Three bedrooms

— Two full and one half baths

■ A one story country-style Ranch with a contemporary floor plan

■ A corner fireplace adding warmth to the Living Room

■ A formal Dining Room with sliding glass doors to the deck

■ An eating bar and Nook area in the Kitchen

■ A vaulted ceiling with skylights in the Family Room

■ A Master Suite with private bath and a cedar closet as well as a walk-in closet

■ Two additional bedrooms that share a full bath

MAIN AREA — 1,998 SQ. FT.
BASEMENT — 1,998 SQ. FT.
GARAGE — 635 SQ. FT.
WIDTH — 87'-0"
DEPTH — 48'-0"

TOTAL LIVING AREA:
1,998 SQ. FT.

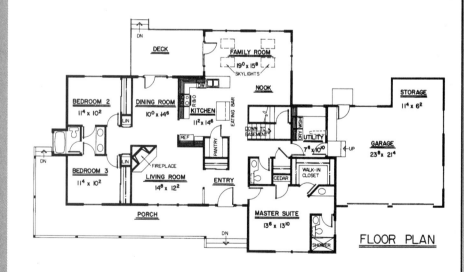

FLOOR PLAN

PRICE CODE A

FOR AN ESTABLISHED NEIGHBORHOOD

No. 93222

■ This plan features:

— Three bedrooms

— Two full baths

■ A covered entrance sheltering and welcoming visitors

■ An expansive Living Room enhanced by natural light streaming in from the large front window

■ A bayed formal Dining Room with direct access to the Sun Deck and the Living Room for entertainment ease

■ An efficient, galley Kitchen equipped with a double sink

■ An informal Breakfast Room

■ A large Master Suite equipped with a walk-in closet and a full private Bath

■ Two additional bedrooms that share a full hall bath

MAIN AREA — 1,276 SQ. FT.
FINISHED STAIRCASE — 16 SQ. FT.
BASEMENT — 392 SQ. FT.
GARAGE — 728 SQ. FT.

TOTAL LIVING AREA:
1,292 SQ. FT.

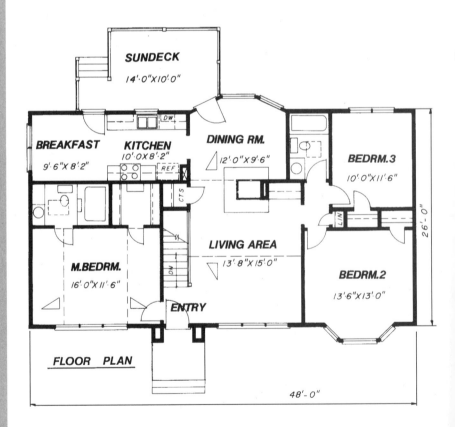

FLOOR PLAN

An
EXCLUSIVE DESIGN
By Jannis Vann & Associates, Inc.

PRICE CODE A

FOR TODAY'S SOPHISTICATED HOMEOWNER

No. 93027

■ This plan features:

— Three bedrooms

— Two full baths

■ A formal Dining Room that opens off the foyer and has a classic bay window

■ A Kitchen notable for it's angled eating bar that opens to the Living Room

■ A cozy fireplace in the Living Room that can be seen from the Kitchen

■ A Master Suite that includes a whirlpool tub/shower combination and a walk-in closet

■ Ten foot ceilings in the major living areas, including the Master Bedroom

MAIN AREA — 1,500 SQ. FT.
GARAGE — 437 SQ. FT.

**TOTAL LIVING AREA:
1,500 SQ. FT.**

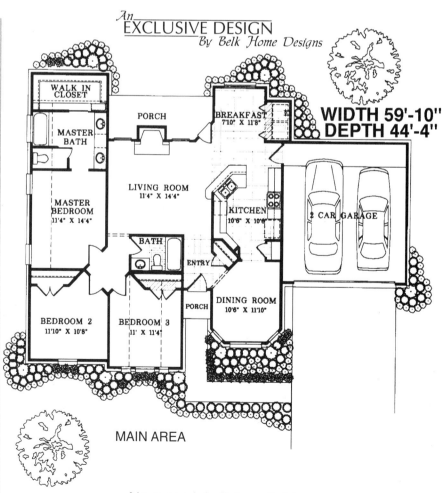

An
EXCLUSIVE DESIGN
By Belk Home Designs

WIDTH 59'-10"
DEPTH 44'-4"

WALK IN CLOSET

PORCH

BREAKFAST
7'10" X 11'8"

MASTER BATH

LIVING ROOM
11'4" X 14'4"

KITCHEN
10'6" X 10'6"

2 CAR GARAGE

MASTER BEDROOM
11'4" X 14'4"

BATH

ENTRY

BEDROOM 2
11'10" X 10'8"

BEDROOM 3
11' X 11'4"

PORCH

DINING ROOM
10'6" X 11'10"

PORCH

MAIN AREA

No materials list available

PRICE CODE C

DISTINCTIVE EUROPEAN DESIGN

No. 92516

■ This plan features:

— Three bedrooms

— Two full baths

■ A spacious Foyer leading into a grand Living Room, topped by a vaulted ceiling, a fireplace between built-in cabinets and a wall of glass leading to a covered Porch

■ A gourmet Kitchen with a peninsula counter/snackbar and a built-in pantry, that is central to the Dining Room, the bay window Breakfast area, the Utility Room and the Garage

■ A large Master Bedroom, crowned by a raised ceiling, with French doors leading to a covered Porch, a luxurious bath and a walk-in closet

MAIN FLOOR — 1,887 SQ. FT.
GARAGE & STORAGE — 524 SQ. FT.

TOTAL LIVING AREA:
1,887 SQ. FT.

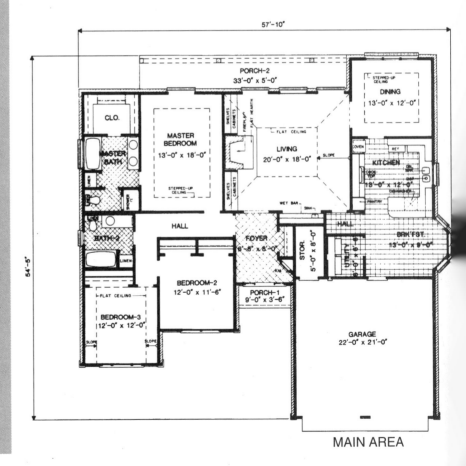

MAIN AREA

PRICE CODE C

STEP-SAVING CONVENIENCE

No. 92617

■ This plan features:

— Three bedrooms

— Two full baths

■ A covered Porch leading into the Foyer

■ A corner fireplace and a wall of windows with an atrium door to the Patio in the Great Room

■ An efficient Kitchen with a built-in pantry, a peninsula counter/snack bar separating it from the Breakfast alcove

■ Topped by a tray ceiling, a private Master Bedroom offers an ultra bath with a walk-in closet, a double vanity and a window tub

■ Two additional bedrooms, one with a sloped ceiling, sharing a full hall bath

MAIN FLOOR — 1,955 SQ. FT.
WIDTH — 58'-2"
DEPTH — 57'-5"

TOTAL LIVING AREA:
1,955 SQ. FT.

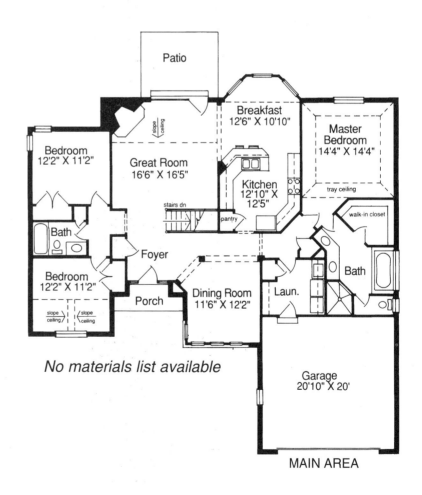

No materials list available

MAIN AREA

PRICE CODE C

CATHEDRAL WINDOWS GRACED BY MASSIVE ARCH

No. 20066

■ This plan features:

— Three bedrooms

— Two full baths

■ A tiled threshold providing a distinctive entrance

■ A comfortable Living Room with a wood-burning fireplace and tiled hearth

■ A Dining Room with vaulted ceiling

■ A Kitchen with central work island, pantry, planning desk, and Breakfast area

■ A Master Suite with decorative ceilings, Master Bath and bow window

FIRST FLOOR — 1,850 SQ. FT.
BASEMENT — 1,850 SQ. FT.
GARAGE — 503 SQ. FT.

TOTAL LIVING AREA:
1,850 SQ. FT.

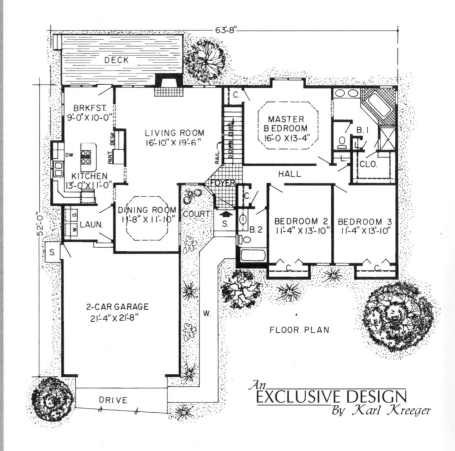

An
EXCLUSIVE DESIGN
By Karl Kreeger

PRICE CODE B

ZONED FOR COMFORT

No. 90610

■ This plan features:

— Three bedrooms

— Two full baths

■ A spacious Kitchen with a built-in pantry, ample cabinet and counter space and a sunny Breakfast area

■ A large Family Room with a fireplace and sliding doors to a covered porch

■ A Master Suite with a walk-in closet and a private Bath

■ Two additional bedrooms with ample closet space and access to the full hall bath

■ A Dining and Living Room laid out for ease in entertaining

FIRST FLOOR — 1,771 SQ. FT.

**TOTAL LIVING AREA:
1,771 SQ. FT.**

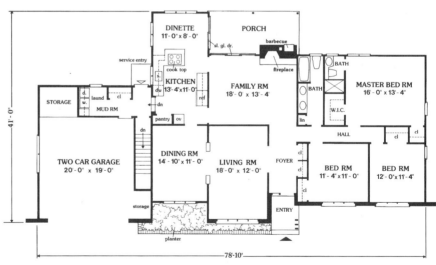

MAIN AREA

PRICE CODE A

AN EARTH SHELTERED HOME

No. 99745

■ This plan features:

— Two bedrooms

— Two full baths

■ The living spaces are placed all on the open side

■ A combined Kitchen/Living/Dining Room, with a semicircle of tall windows, catching light from three sides

■ The Kitchen counters, sitting at the hinge of two wall angles, make a lazy bend to create space for a media nook and pantry

■ A luxurious Master Suite having an oversized tub, walk-in closet, and vanity with a skylight in the ceiling

■ An additional bedroom, with sky-lights, that has easy access to a full hall bath

MAIN AREA — 1,482 SQ. FT.
GARAGE — 564 SQ. FT.

TOTAL LIVING AREA:
1,482 SQ. FT.

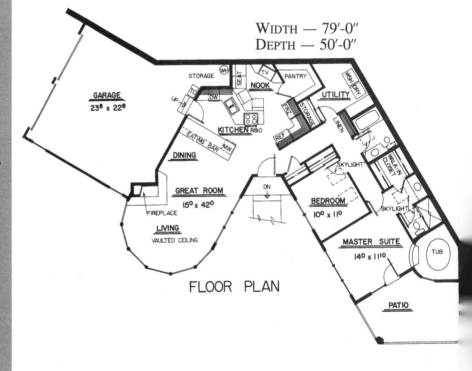

WIDTH — 79'-0"
DEPTH — 50'-0"

FLOOR PLAN

PRICE CODE A

No. 99710

■ This plan features:

— Three bedrooms

— Two full baths

■ Lofty brick columns flanking the high gabled entryway

■ A large corner fireplace in the Great Room which can be enjoyed from both the Dining Room and the Kitchen

■ An efficient wrap-around Kitchen with many built-ins, opening via an eating bar, to the Great Room and Dining Room

■ A privately situated Master Suite, complete with a full bath and a walk-in closet

■ Two additional bedrooms that share a full hall bath

■ Utility room, accessed from the garage, also serves as a Laundry Room

MAIN AREA — 1,459 SQ. FT.
GARAGE — 567 SQ. FT.
WIDTH — 56'-0"
DEPTH — 54'-0"

TOTAL LIVING AREA:
1,459 SQ. FT.

STATELY AND SPACIOUS CONTEMPORARY

MAIN AREA

An
EXCLUSIVE DESIGN
By Landmark Designs, Inc.

PRICE CODE C

BRICK ARCHWAY ACCENTS ENTRANCE

No. 93010

■ This plan features:

— Three bedrooms

— Two full baths

■ An expansive Great Room with arched entrance, supported by square columns, adding to the elegance of the room

■ An efficient Kitchen with corner double sink and cooktop island

■ A sunny Breakfast area, flowing off of the Kitchen

■ A spacious Master Suite with a bay window and private bath

■ Two additional bedrooms with walk-in closets that share a full hall bath

FIRST FLOOR — 1,985 SQ. FT.
GARAGE — 463 SQ. FT.
WIDTH — 71'-0"
DEPTH — 57'-0"

**TOTAL LIVING AREA:
1,985 SQ. FT.**

No materials list available

An
EXCLUSIVE DESIGN
By Belk Home Designs

PRICE CODE B

STYLISH CLASSIC

No. 93008

■ This plan features:

— Three bedrooms

— Two full baths

■ An open layout

■ A Breakfast area and Great Room that creates a feeling of spaciousness

■ An efficient Kitchen layout to conveniently serve both formal and informal eating areas

■ An impressive Master Suite including sloped ceilings, walk-in closet and private Master Bath

MAIN AREA — 1,578 SQ. FT.
GARAGE — 439 SQ. FT.
PORCH — 41 SQ. FT.
WIDTH — 55'-6"
DEPTH — 52'-0"

TOTAL LIVING AREA:
1,578 SQ. FT.

No materials list available

An
EXCLUSIVE DESIGN
By Belk Home Designs

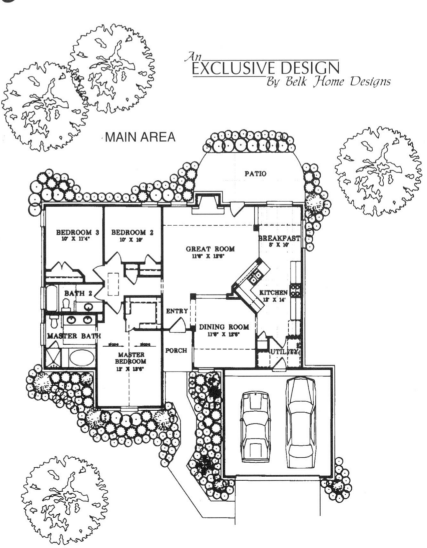

MAIN AREA

PRICE CODE A

ATTRACTIVE ROOF LINES

No. 90983

■ This plan features:

— Three bedrooms

— Two full baths

■ An open floor plan shared by the sunken Living Room, Dining and Kitchen areas

■ An unfinished daylight Basement which will provide future bedrooms, a bathroom and laundry facilities

■ A Master Suite with a big walk-in closet and a private bath featuring a double shower

FIRST FLOOR — 1,396 SQ. FT.
BASEMENT — 1,396 SQ. FT.
GARAGE — 389 SQ. FT.
WIDTH — 48'-0"
DEPTH — 54'-0"

TOTAL LIVING AREA:
1,396 SQ. FT.

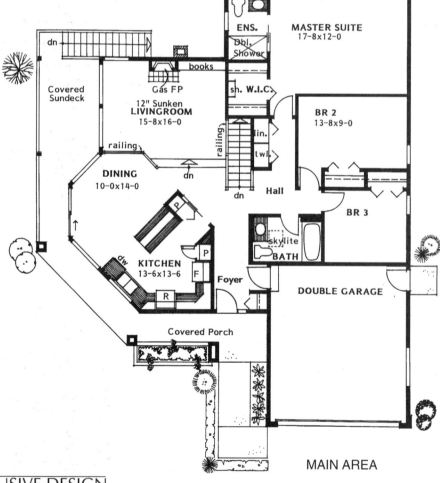

An
EXCLUSIVE DESIGN
By Westhome Planners, Ltd.

PRICE CODE A

CHARMING SOUTHERN TRADITIONAL

No. 92503

■ This plan features:

— Three bedrooms

— Two full baths

■ A covered front porch with striking columns, brick quoins, and dental molding

■ A spacious Great Room with vaulted ceilings, a fireplace, and built-in cabinets

■ A Utility Room adjacent to the Kitchen, which leads to the two-car Garage and Storage Rooms

■ A Master Bedroom including a large walk-in closet and a compartmentalized bath

MAIN AREA — 1,271 SQ. FT.
GARAGE — 506 SQ. FT.

TOTAL LIVING AREA:
1,271 SQ. FT.

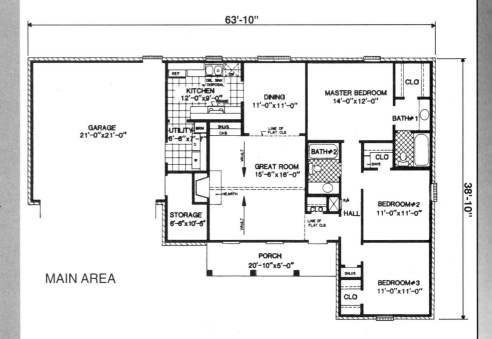

MAIN AREA

PRICE CODE D

CENTRAL ATRIUM HIGHLIGHTS PLAN

No. 10464

■ This plan features:

— Three bedrooms

— Two and a half baths

■ A tiled entry hall continuing into the Family Room offers easy maintenance and access to all the living areas and the Garage

■ A unique Atrium in the center of the home offers outdoor living inside

■ A spacious Living Room with a fireplace flanked by bookcases

■ An efficient Kitchen featuring a peninsula counter/snackbar dividing the Family Room, Nook and Utility areas

■ A Master Bedroom suite offering a plush, double vanity bath

■ Two additional bedrooms with walk-in closets and private access to a full bath

MAIN FLOOR — 2,222 SQ. FT.
GARAGE — 468 SQ. FT.

TOTAL LIVING AREA:
2,222 SQ. FT.

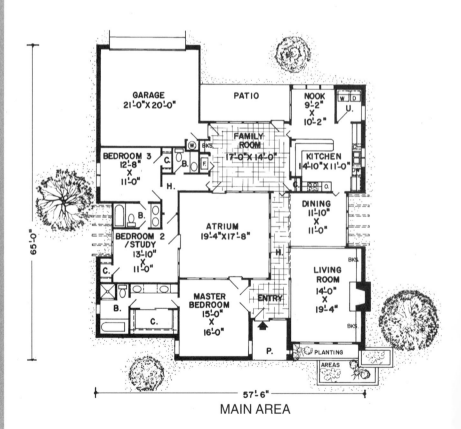

MAIN AREA

PRICE CODE A

LOW MAINTENANCE, SOUTHWESTERN STYLE

No. 10643

- ◼ This plan features:
- — Three bedrooms
- — Two full baths
- ◼ A stucco facade with an arched privacy wall, leading into a tiled entrance
- ◼ An airy Living Room providing easy entertaining and access to other areas
- ◼ A central Kitchen equipped with a cooktop island/breakfast bar, adjoining the Dining Room
- ◼ A Master Suite offering a bay window area, a walk-in closet and a private bath with a skylight
- ◼ Two additional bedrooms with oversized closets sharing a full hall bath

MAIN FLOOR — 1,285 SQ. FT.
GARAGE — 473 SQ. FT.

TOTAL LIVING AREA:
1,285 SQ. FT.

An
EXCLUSIVE DESIGN
By Karl Kreeger

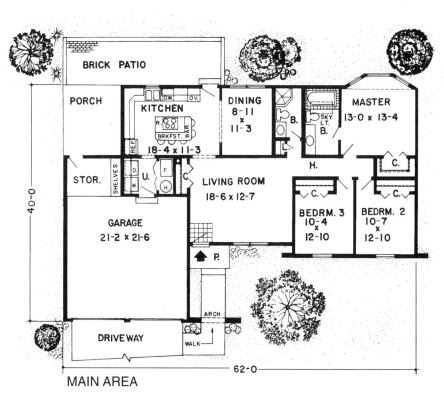

PRICE CODE A

ATTRACTIVE DETAILING ADDS IMPRESSIVE STYLE

No. 93007

■ This plan features:

— Three bedrooms

— Two full baths

■ A Master Bedroom with decorative ceiling and private Master Bath

■ A spacious, fireplaced Great Room as the center of the home, with easy access to the patio

■ An efficient Kitchen with peninsula counter area and ample storage space

MAIN AREA — 1,429 SQ. FT.
GARAGE — 456 SQ. FT.
PORCH — 29 SQ. FT.
WIDTH — 51'-10"
DEPTH — 40'-10"

TOTAL LIVING AREA:
1,429 SQ. FT.

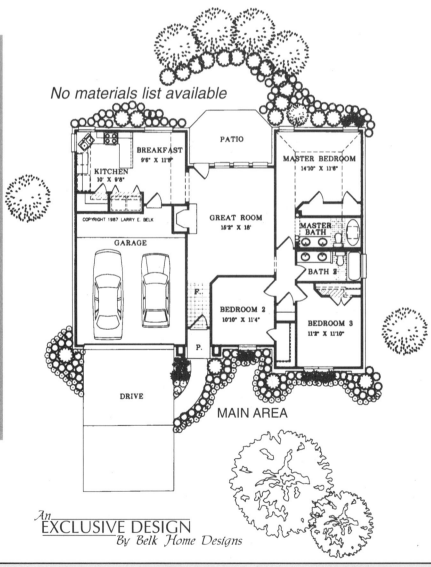

No materials list available

MAIN AREA

An
EXCLUSIVE DESIGN
By Belk Home Designs

PRICE CODE A

A LOVELY SMALL HOME

No. 93026

■ This plan features:

— Three bedrooms

— Two full baths

■ A large Living Room with a ten foot ceiling

■ A Dining Room with a distinctive bay window

■ A Breakfast Room located off the Kitchen

■ A Kitchen with an angled eating bar to open that opens the room to the Living Room

■ A Master Suite with ten foot ceiling and his-n-her vanities, a combination whirlpool tub and shower, plus a huge walk-in closet

■ Two additional bedrooms that share a full bath

MAIN AREA — 1,402 SQ. FT.
GARAGE — 437 SQ. FT.

TOTAL LIVING AREA:
1,402 SQ. FT.

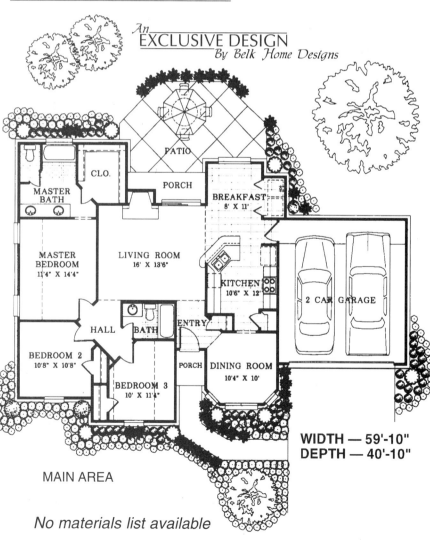

An EXCLUSIVE DESIGN
By Belk Home Designs

MAIN AREA

WIDTH — 59'-10"
DEPTH — 40'-10"

No materials list available

PRICE CODE C

ROOF GARDEN DELIGHT

An EXCLUSIVE DESIGN
By Marshall Associates

No. 94304

■ This plan features:

— Three bedrooms

— Two full baths

■ A tiled Entry Court leading into the Foyer and setting a southwestern theme

■ A Living/Dining area with a corner fireplace, window walls and access to a Patio

■ An efficient, U-shaped Kitchen with an eating bar and laundry area

■ Two first floor bedrooms sharing a full bath

■ A second floor Master Bedroom with a double closet, built-in shelves, a private bath and direct access to the Roof Garden

FIRST FLOOR — 981 SQ. FT.
SECOND FLOOR — 396 SQ. FT.

**TOTAL LIVING AREA:
1,377 SQ. FT.**

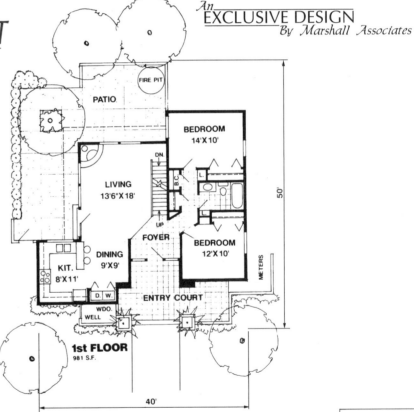

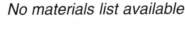

No materials list available

PRICE CODE B

GREEK REVIVAL

No. 99610

■ This plan features:

— Three bedrooms

— Two full baths

■ A large front porch with pediment and columns

■ A stunning, heat-circulating fireplace flanked by cabinetry and shelves in the Living Room

■ A formal Dining Room enhanced by a bay window

■ An efficient, U-shaped Kitchen with a peninsula counter and informal Dinette area

■ A Master Suite with a private Master Bath and direct access to the private terrace

■ Two additional bedrooms sharing a full hall bath

FIRST FLOOR — 1,460 SQ. FT.
LAUNDRY/MUDROOM — 68 SQ. FT.
BASEMENT — 1,367 SQ. FT.
GARAGE & STORAGE — 494 SQ. FT.

TOTAL LIVING AREA:
1,528 SQ. FT.

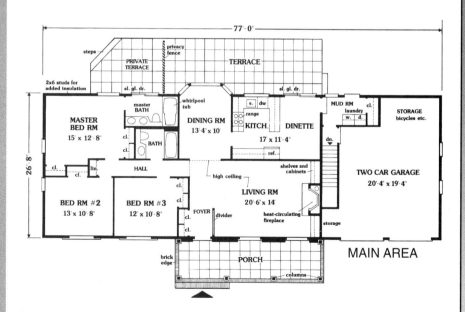

PRICE CODE B

WIDE OPEN LIVING AREAS

No. 91814

■ This plan features:

— Three bedrooms

— Two full baths

■ Adaptable for barrier-free living

■ An efficient Kitchen with double sink peninsula counter, that also serves as an eating bar

■ A covered Porch and a patio with decorative columns and half-round windows

■ A large Master Bedroom with a patio, double sinks, walk-in closet, spa tub, and a shower

■ Two additional bedrooms that share a full hall bath

■ An optional crawl space or slab foundation — please specify when ordering

MAIN AREA — 1,785 SQ. FT.
GARAGE — 672 SQ. FT.

**TOTAL LIVING AREA:
1,785 SQ. FT.**

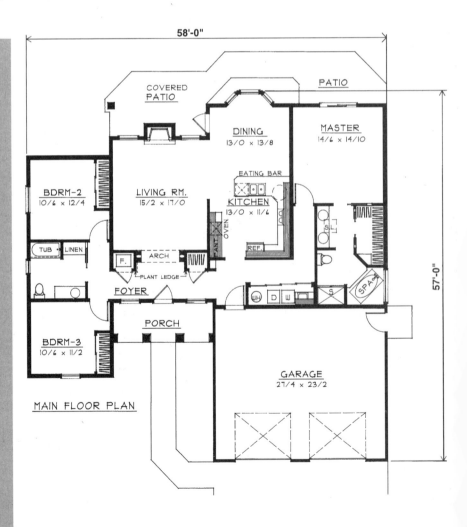

MAIN FLOOR PLAN

PRICE CODE A

AFFORDABLE ENERGY-SAVER

No. 90680

■ This plan features:

— Three bedrooms

— Two full baths

■ A covered Porch leading into an open Foyer and Living/Dining Room with skylights and front to back exposure

■ An efficient Kitchen with a bay window Dinette area, a walk-in Pantry and adjacent to the Mud Room, Garage area

■ A private Master Bedroom with a luxurious Master Bath leading to a private Deck complete with a Hot Tub

■ Two additional bedrooms with access to a full hall bath

MAIN FLOOR — 1,393 SQ. FT.
BASEMENT — 1,393 SQ. FT.

TOTAL LIVING AREA:
1,393 SQ. FT.

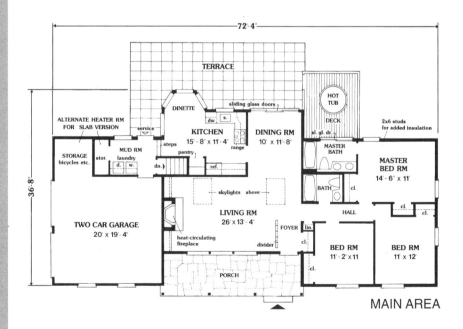

MAIN AREA

PRICE CODE B

PERFECT FOR A FIRST HOME

No. 92405

■ This plan features:

— Three bedrooms

— Two full baths

■ A spacious Master Suite including a separate Master Bath with a garden tub and shower

■ A Dining Room and Family Room highlighted by vaulted ceilings

■ An oversized patio accessible from the Master Suite, Family Room and Breakfast Room

■ A well planned Kitchen measuring 12' x 11'

MAIN AREA — 1,564 SQ. FT.
GARAGE & STORAGE — 476 SQ. FT.

TOTAL LIVING AREA:
1,564 SQ. FT.

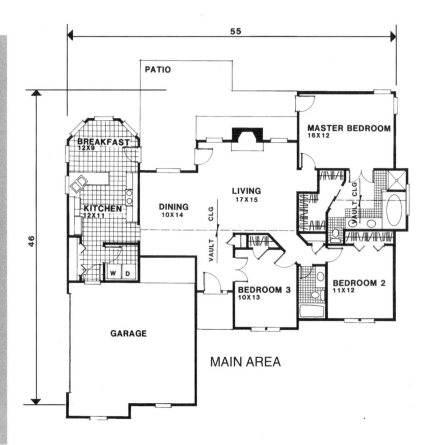

MAIN AREA

No materials list available

PRICE CODE B

SECLUDED MASTER SUITE

No. 92527

■ This plan features:

— Three bedrooms

— Two full baths

■ A convenient one-level design with an open floor plan between the Kitchen, Breakfast area and Great Room

■ A vaulted ceiling and a cozy fire-place in the spacious Great Room

■ A well-equipped Kitchen using a peninsula counter as an eating bar

■ A Master Suite with a luxurious Master Bath

■ Two additional bedrooms having use of a full hall bath

MAIN AREA — 1,680 SQ. FT.

**TOTAL LIVING AREA:
1,680 SQ. FT.**

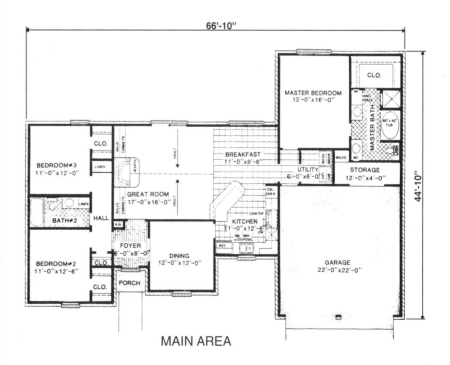

MAIN AREA

PRICE CODE C

CENTRAL COURTYARD FEATURES POOL

No. 10507

■ This plan features:

— Three bedrooms

— Two baths

■ A central courtyard complete with a pool

■ A secluded Master Bedroom accented by a skylight, a spacious walk-in closet, and a private bath

■ A convenient Kitchen easily serving the patio for comfortable outdoor entertaining

■ A detached two-car Garage

FIRST FLOOR — 2,194 SQ. FT.
GARAGE — 576 SQ. FT.

**TOTAL LIVING AREA:
2,194 SQ. FT.**

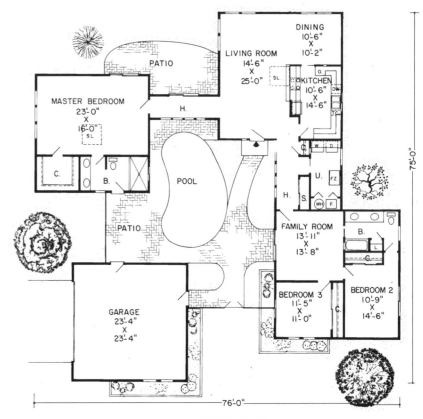

MAIN AREA

PRICE CODE D

DOUBLE DOORS GIVE A SPANISH WELCOME

No. 10108

■ This plan features:

— Three bedrooms

— Two full and one half baths

■ Massive double doors opening to the foyer

■ A 27-foot Living Room to the right of the foyer

■ A large Master Bedroom with a walk-in closet and a private full bath

FIRST FLOOR — 1,176 SQ. FT.
SECOND FLOOR — 1,176 SQ. FT.
BASEMENT — 1,176 SQ. FT.
GARAGE — 576 SQ. FT.

**TOTAL LIVING AREA:
2,352 SQ. FT.**

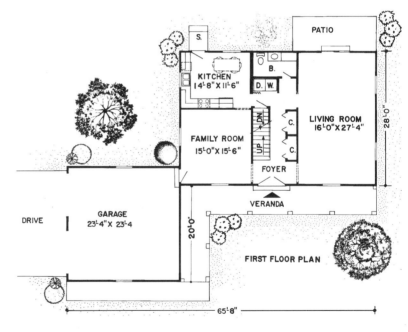

FIRST FLOOR PLAN

SECOND FLOOR PLAN

PRICE CODE B

ENHANCED BY A COLUMNED PORCH

No. 92531

■ This plan features:

— Three bedrooms

— Two full baths

■ A Great Room with a fireplace and decorative ceiling

■ A large efficient Kitchen with Breakfast area

■ A Master Bedroom with a private Master Bath and walk-in closet

■ A formal Dining Room conveniently located near the Kitchen

■ Two additional bedrooms with walk-in closets and use of full hall bath

FIRST FLOOR — 1,754 SQ. FT.

TOTAL LIVING AREA:
1,754 SQ. FT.

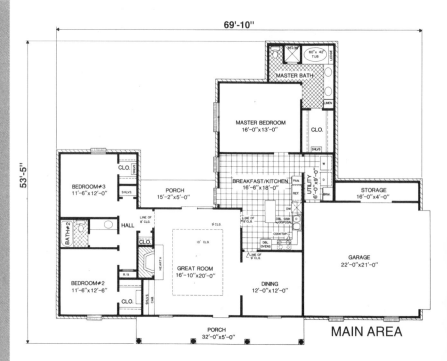

PRICE CODE B

SPECTACULAR RAMBLER

No. 91811

■ This plan features:

— Three bedrooms

— Two full baths

■ A twelve foot ceiling over the Foyer, Living Room, Kitchen and Dining Rooms

■ A sunken Living Room with custom-cut windows

■ A spacious Master Suite with a walk-in closet, and a private bath

■ A Family Room with a fireplace, separated from the Kitchen by an eating bar

■ An efficient Kitchen with a double sink, built-in pantry, and a peninsula counter

■ An optional basement, slab or crawl space foundation — please specify when ordering

MAIN AREA — 1,546 SQ. FT.
OPTIONAL BASEMENT — 1,588 SQ. FT.
GARAGE — 549 SQ. FT.

TOTAL LIVING AREA:
1,546 SQ. FT.

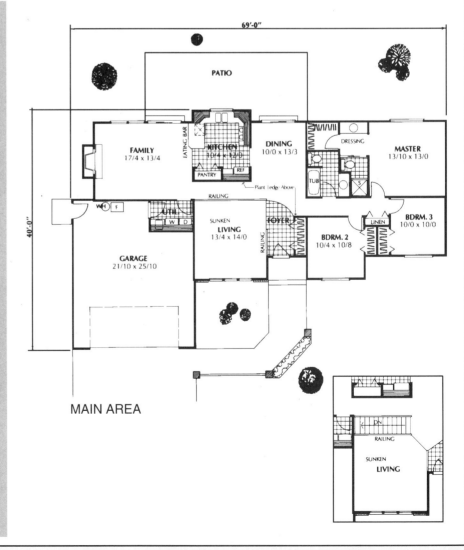

MAIN AREA

PRICE CODE B

SKYLIGHT WELCOME

No. 90695

■ This plan features:

— Three bedrooms

— Two full baths

■ A covered, double door entrance into the Foyer, with skylights, opening to the Living Room/Dining Room

■ A heat-circulating fireplace with an extended hearth in the Living Room, enhanced by a wall of glass and a sliding door to the Terrace in the Dining Room

■ A centrally-located Kitchen/Dinette with a skylight, a sliding glass door to the Sun Room

■ A Family Room with a built-in media center, more windows and a sliding glass door to the Terrace

■ A Master Bedroom suite with a walk-in closet, and a private bath with a whirlpool tub

■ Two additional bedrooms sharing a full hall bath

MAIN FLOOR — 1,726 SQ. FT.

TOTAL LIVING AREA:
1,726 SQ. FT.

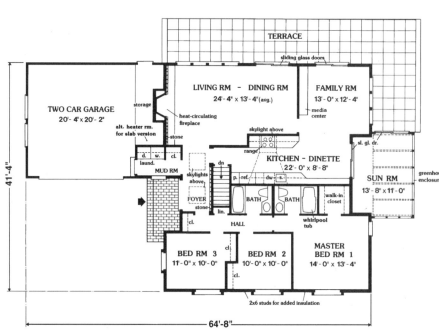

MAIN AREA

PRICE CODE B

FIREPLACE IS CENTER OF CIRCULAR LIVING AREA

No. 10274

■ This plan features:

— Three bedrooms

— Two full baths

■ A dramatically positioned fireplace as a focal point for the main living area

■ The Kitchen, Dining and Living Rooms form a circle that allows work areas to flow into living areas

■ Sliding glass doors accessible to wood a Deck

■ A convenient Laundry Room located off the Kitchen

■ A double Garage providing excellent storage

■ Accessibility Features:

— Level entry way

— Wide doorways (32"-36" clear width)

— Chair height electrical controls/outlets

— Reinforced walls for installation of grab bars

FIRST FLOOR — 1,783 SQ. FT.
GARAGE — 576 SQ. FT.

TOTAL LIVING AREA:
1,783 SQ. FT.

PRICE CODE A

SPANISH STYLING, AFFORDABLE DESIGN

No. 91340

■ This plan features:

— Two bedrooms

— Two full baths

■ A large Master Suite with vaulted ceilings and a handicap accessible private bath

■ Vaulted ceilings in the Great Room

■ An open Kitchen area with an eating bar

■ Accessibility Features:

— Level entry way

— Wide doorways (32"-36" clear width)

— Chair height electrical controls/outlets

— Reinforced walls for installation of grab bars

MAIN AREA — 1,111 SQ. FT.

TOTAL LIVING AREA:
1,111 SQ. FT.

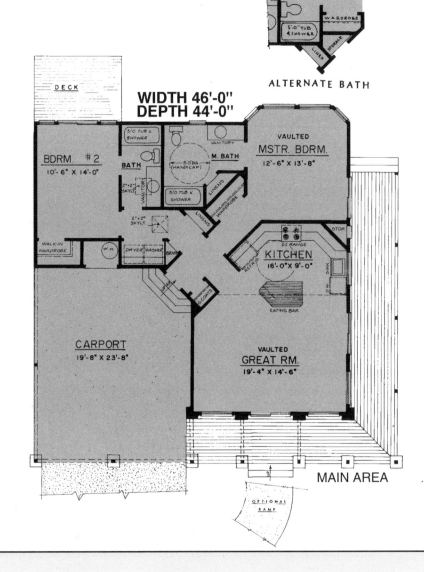

ALTERNATE BATH

WIDTH 46'-0"
DEPTH 44'-0"

PRICE CODE C

CAREFREE AND COZY

An
EXCLUSIVE DESIGN
By Mark Stewart

No. 91618

■ This plan features:

— Three bedrooms

— Two full and one half baths

■ A coved ceiling, fireplace and massive front window in the Living Room

■ A built-in, corner china cabinet in the elegant, formal Dining Room

■ A Kitchen with a large cook top island and snack counter

■ A secluded Master Suite with a bay window, coved ceiling, and a private bath with double vanities and garden spa tub

■ Accessibility Features:

— Level entry way

— Wide doorways (32"-36" clear width)

— Chair height electrical controls/outlets

— Reinforced walls for installation of grab bars

FIRST FLOOR — 2,087 SQ. FT.

TOTAL LIVING AREA:
2,087 SQ. FT.

MAIN FLOOR

No materials list available

PRICE CODE C

No. 20402

CAREFREE CONVENIENCE

■ This plan features:

— Three bedrooms

— Two full baths

■ A covered Porch leading into the open Living Room and Dining area with a wooden Deck beyond

■ Kitchen with a roll-out pantry, knee space under the counter and an open counter connecting the Family Room

■ Adjacent to the Kitchen, a Breakfast area with windows on three sides and ramped Garage

■ A spacious Master Bedroom with access to the Deck, plush bath and over-sized closet

■ Accessibility Features

— Level entry way

— Wide doorways (32"-36")

— Chair height electrical controls/outlets

— Reinforced walls for installation of grab bars

MAIN FLOOR — 2,153 SQ. FT.
GARAGE — 617 SQ. FT.
PORCH —210 SQ. FT.

TOTAL LIVING AREA:
2,153 SQ. FT.

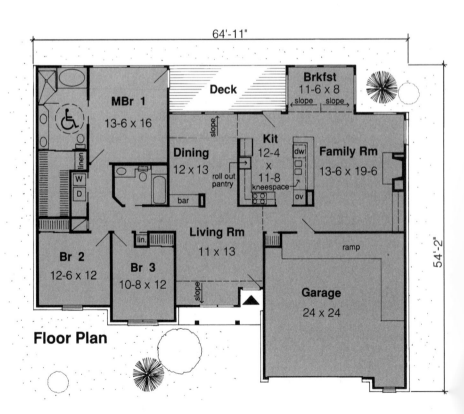

Floor Plan

PRICE CODE B

RANCH WITH HANDICAPPED ACCESS

No. 20403

■ This plan features:

— Three bedrooms

— Two full baths

■ Ramps into the front Entry from the Porch; the Utility area and the Kitchen from the Garage; and the Family Room from the Deck

■ An efficient Kitchen with a built-in pantry and an open counter.

■ A Master Bedroom suite offering access to the Deck, closet and bath

■ Accessibility Features:

— Level entry way

— Wide doorways (32″-36″)

— Chair height electrical controls/outlets

— Reinforced walls for installation of grab bars

MAIN FLOOR — 1,734 SQ. FT.
PORCH — 118 SQ. FT.
DECK — 354 SQ. FT.
GARAGE — 606 SQ. FT.

TOTAL LIVING AREA:
1,734 SQ. FT.

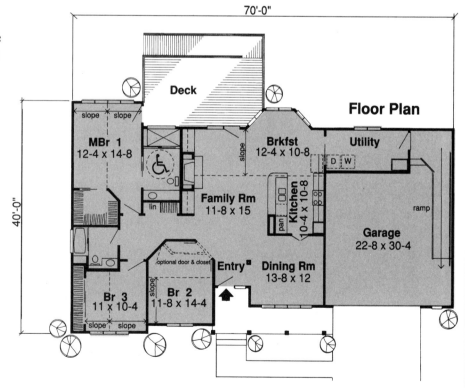

Floor Plan

PRICE CODE D

No. 91623

■ This plan features:

— Three bedrooms

— Two full and one half baths

■ A covered Entry with easy maintenance tile continuing into the Kitchen and the Garage

■ Coved ceilings in the Living, Dining and Master bedroom suite adding elegant feeling of space

■ An efficient Kitchen with an island cooktop and a serving bar for eating

■ A lower level Family Room with a wall of windows and sliding glass doors

■ Accessibility Features:

— Level entry way

— Wide doorways (32"-36" clear width)

— Chair height electrical controls/outlets

— Reinforced walls for installation of grab bars

FIRST FLOOR — 2,087 SQ. FT.
MAIN FLOOR — 1,418 SQ. FT.
LOWER FLOOR — 1,054 SQ. FT.

TOTAL LIVING AREA:
2,472 SQ. FT.

HILLSIDE HAVEN

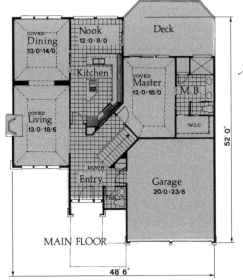

MAIN FLOOR

An
EXCLUSIVE DESIGN
By Mark Stewart

No materials list available

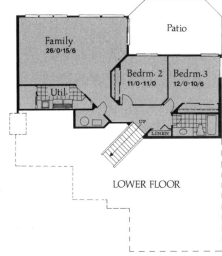

LOWER FLOOR

PRICE CODE A

No. 91646

■ This plan features:

— Three bedrooms

— Two full baths

■ A wide, window Entry into the open layout of the Living/Dining Room and the Kitchen, and French doors into the Den

■ A efficient Kitchen with a corner window and sink, a peninsula cooktop counter to serve the Dining area, and adjoining the Utility room and the Garage

■ A Master suite with French doors, decorative windows, two accesses to an oversized closet and a private bath with a roll-in shower

■ Two additional bedrooms with double closets, sharing a full hall bath

■ Accessibility Features:

— Level entry way

— Wide doorways (32"-36" clear width)

— Chair height electrical controls/outlets

— Reinforced walls for installation of grab bars

MAIN FLOOR — 1,422 SQ. FT.

DISTINCTIVE FEATURES

TOTAL LIVING AREA:
1,422 SQ. FT.

DINING
11/0X10/0

MASTER
14/0X12/0

LIVING
12/6X14/0

ROLL IN
SHWR

GRAB
BARS

KITCHEN

GRAB
BARS

ENTRY

BED 2
10/6X10/0

BED 3
10/0X10/0

DEN
12/0X10/0

UTIL

SELF CLOSER

50'0"

MAIN FLOOR

GARAGE
20/0X19/6

50'0"

An
EXCLUSIVE DESIGN
By Mark Stewart

PRICE CODE A

No. 91647

- ■ This plan features:
- — Two bedrooms
- — Two full baths
- ■ A tiled Entry leading into the Living/Dining area and the Family Room
- ■ A cozy fireplace warming both the Living and the Dining areas
- ■ A convenient Kitchen with a serving bar to the Family Room and next to the Dining Room
- ■ French doors into the Master suite with a spacious closet and a private bath offering a double vanity and a roll-in shower
- ■ A second bedroom with a double closet adjacent to a full bath
- ■ Accessibility Features:
- — Level entry way
- — Wide doorways (32"-36" clear width)
- — Chair height electrical controls/outlets
- — Reinforced walls for installation of grab bars

MAIN FLOOR — 1,444 SQ. FT.

TOTAL LIVING AREA:
1,444 SQ. FT.

*I*DEAL FAMILY PLAN

An
EXCLUSIVE DESIGN
By Mark Stewart

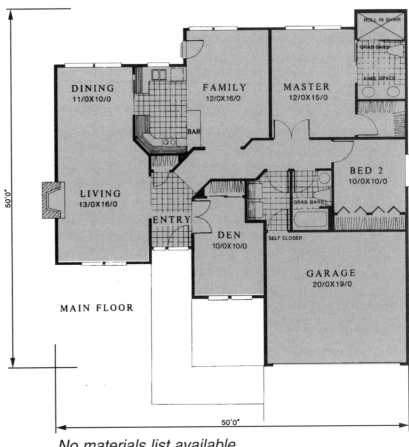

No materials list available

PRICE CODE A

BASIC LIVING DESIGN

No. 91342

■ This plan features:

— Three bedrooms

— Two full baths

■ A handicapped Master Bath plan is available

■ Vaulted Great Room, Dining Room and Kitchen areas

■ A Kitchen accented with angles and an abundance of cabinets for storage

■ A Master Bedroom with an ample sized wardrobe, large covered private deck, and private bath

■ Accessibility Features:

— Level entry way

— Wide doorways (32″-36″ clear width)

— Chair height electrical controls/outlets

— Reinforced walls for installation of grab bars

MAIN AREA — 1,345 SQ. FT.
WIDTH — 47′-8″
DEPTH — 56′-0″

TOTAL LIVING AREA:
1,345 SQ. FT.

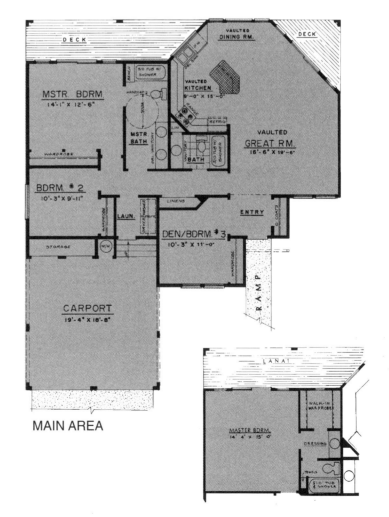

MAIN AREA

ALTERNATE BATH

PRICE CODE B

No. 91651

YOURS FOR AS LIFETIME

■ This plan features:

— Three bedrooms

— Two full baths

■ A vaulted ceiling enhancing the window alcove in the Living Room and corner windows in the Dining area

■ An efficient Kitchen with a peninsula sink serving the Family room and the eating Nook, with a laundry room and access to the Porch

■ A Master suite with an over-sized closet and a private bath with a roll-in shower

■ A Den/Bedroom and a second bedroom sharing a full hall bath

■ Accessibility Features:

— Level entry way

— Wide doorways (32"-36" clear width)

— Chair height electrical controls/outlets

— Reinforced walls for installation of grab bars

MAIN LIVING AREA — 1,653 SQ. FT.

TOTAL LIVING AREA:
1,653 SQ. FT.

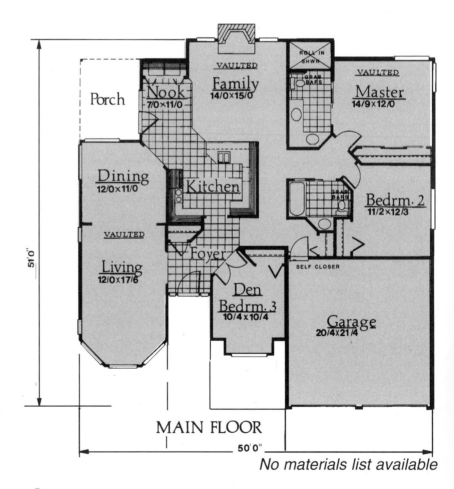

MAIN FLOOR

No materials list available

An
EXCLUSIVE DESIGN
By Mark Stewart

PRICE CODE B

No. 91652

■ This plan features:

— Three bedrooms

— Two full baths

■ A wide tiled Entry leading through the elegant arched doorway into the Living/Dining area with a hearth fireplace and decorative windows

■ A well-designed Kitchen, adjacent to the Dining area, with a corner window and a sink and a peninsula counter serving the Family Room

■ A Master Suite with a sliding glass door to the patio, an over-sized closet and a private bath double vanity and a roll-in shower

■ Two additional bedrooms sharing a full hall bath

■ Accessibility Features:

— Level entry way

— Wide doorways (32"-36" clear width)

— Chair height electrical controls/outlets

— Reinforced walls for installation of grab bars

MAIN FLOOR — 1,541 SQ. FT.

TOTAL LIVING AREA:
1,541 SQ. FT.

ADAPTABLE FOR THE DISABLED

An
EXCLUSIVE DESIGN
By Mark Stewart

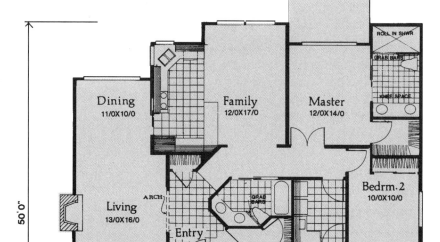

MAIN FLOOR

No materials list available

PRICE CODE C

SELF-SUFFICIENT PLAN FOR THE PHYSICALLY CHALLENGED

No. 10360

■ This plan features:

— Three bedrooms

— Two full baths

■ A ramp walkway to a covered Porch and an open Entry leading into an unusual, octagon-shaped Great Room area, with a central fireplace and direct access to the Patio

■ An efficient, L-shaped Kitchen with a Dinette adjacent to the Dining area.

■ A roomy Master Bedroom, deep closet, a private bath and a separate entrance

■ Accessibility Features:

— Level entry way

— Wide doorways (32″-36″)

— Chair height electrical controls/outlets

— Reinforced walls for installation of grab bars

MAIN FLOOR — 1,882 SQ. FT.
GARAGE — 728 SQ. FT.

TOTAL LIVING AREA:
1,882 SQ. FT.

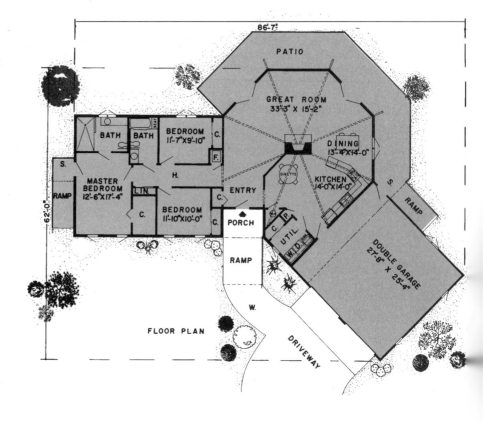

FLOOR PLAN

PRICE CODE A

No. 91341

COMPACT AND CONVENIENT

■ This plan features:

— Two bedrooms

— Two full baths

■ A ramp to a covered Porch, a tiled Foyer and an open layout for the Living Room, the Dining Room, and the Kitchen

■ An angled Living/Dining Room area with large windows and double sliding glass doors to covered Decks with skylights

■ An efficient Kitchen with ample cabinet and counter space, and an island sink/breakfast bar enhanced by two skylights

■ Accessibility Features:

— Level entry way

—Wide doorways (32"-36" clear width)

—Chair height electrical controls/outlets

—Reinforced walls for installation of grab bars

MAIN FLOOR — 1,170 SQ. FT.
WIDTH — 46'-0"
DEPTH — 49'-4"

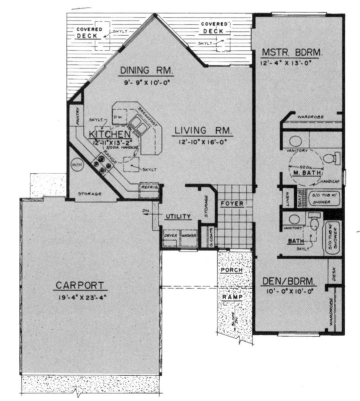

MAIN AREA

ALTERNATE BATH

TOTAL LIVING AREA:
1,170 SQ. FT.

PRICE CODE A

ACCESSIBLE AND AESTHETIC

DESIGN NO. 91683

- This plan features:
- — Three bedrooms
- — Two full baths
- A tiled Entry into an expansive Living/Dining area with a hearth fireplace framed by decorative windows
- An efficient Kitchen and an eating Nook with a built-in pantry adjacent to the Utility room leading to the Garage
- A spacious Master Suite with a wall of windows and a private bath with an over-sized closet and a roll-in shower
- Two additional bedrooms, one with a coved ceiling, sharing a full hall bath
- Accessibility Features:
- — Level entry way
- — Wide doorways (32"-36" clear width)
- — Chair height electrical controls/outlets
- — Reinforced walls for installation of grab bars

MAIN FLOOR — 1,418 SQ. FT.
GARAGE — 390 SQ. FT.

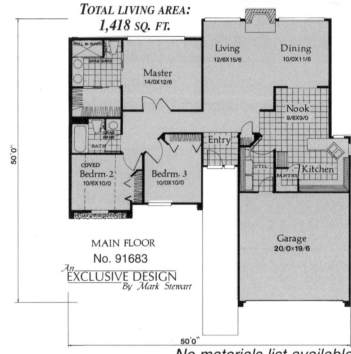

TOTAL LIVING AREA: 1,418 SQ. FT.

MAIN FLOOR
No. 91683

An EXCLUSIVE DESIGN
By Mark Stewart

No materials list available

SIMPLE, YET STYLISH

DESIGN NO. 91653

- This plan features:
- — Three bedrooms
- — Two full baths
- A welcoming arch below a steep roofline leading into the Living/Dining area with columns, a decorative ceiling and a window, a fireplace between built-in shelves and an atrium door to the outdoors
- An L-shaped Kitchen, adjoining the Dining area, with a cooking island opening to the Family Room with a coved ceiling and a sliding glass door to the Patio
- A Master Suite with a private bath, two over-sized closets and a coved ceiling above a decorative window and another sliding glass door to the Patio
- Two additional bedrooms sharing a full hall bath
- An efficient Utility Room leading to the Garage

An EXCLUSIVE DESIGN
By Mark Stewart

- Accessibility Features:
- — Level entry way
- — Wide doorways (32"-36" clear width)
- — Chair height electrical controls/outlets
- — Reinforced walls for installation of grab bars

MAIN FLOOR — 1,889 SQ. FT.

TOTAL LIVING AREA: 1,889 SQ. FT.

No. 91653 MAIN FLOOR

PRICE CODE F

A LIFETIME HOME

DESIGN NO. 91662

This plan features:

— Five bedrooms

— Three full baths

A design that can be modified to accommodate permanently disabled individuals

Wider hallways, doors, and low profile thresholds

A Master Suite with a coved ceiling and Master Bath with a roll-in shower and grab bars appropriately placed

A vaulted ceiling in the Great Room with a fireplace

An island Kitchen with a built-in pantry and sunny eating Nook

A coved ceiling, and an abundance of windows in the front bedroom

A large Recreational Room in the finished Basement

Accessibility Features:

- Level entry way
- Wide doorways (32″-36″ clear width)
- Chair height electrical controls/outlets
- Reinforced walls for installation of grab bars

MAIN FLOOR
No. 91662

LOWER FLOOR

FIRST FLOOR — 2,167 SQ. FT.
FINISHED BASEMENT — 1,154 SQ. FT.

TOTAL LIVING AREA:
3,321 SQ. FT.

An
EXCLUSIVE DESIGN
By Mark Stewart

PRICE CODE C

ROOM TO GROW

DESIGN NO. 91628

- This plan features:
- — Four bedrooms
- — Two full and one half baths
- A open Foyer leading into the bright Living Room with a vaulted ceiling above the decorative corner windows
- An L-shaped Kitchen with a pantry, a built-in desk and an island cooktop serving bar serving the Dining, Family and glass eating Nook
- A cozy Family Room with a huge fireplace between two windows and a sliding glass door to the Deck
- A Master Suite with an over-sized closet and a plush Master Bath including a spa and a roll-in shower
- Three additional bedrooms with ample closets, sharing a full hall bath
- A Bonus area over the Garage to finish now, or later
- Accessibility Features:
- — Level entry way
- — Wide doorways (32"-36" clear width)
- — Chair height electrical controls/outlets
- — Reinforced walls for installation of grab bars

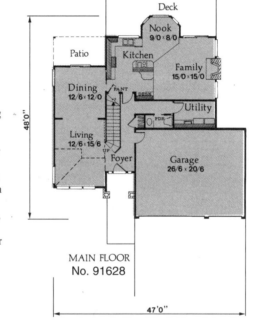

MAIN FLOOR
No. 91628

FIRST FLOOR — 1,085 SQ. FT.
SECOND FLOOR — 941 SQ. FT.
BONUS — 238 SQ. FT.

TOTAL LIVING AREA:
2,026 SQ. FT.

An
EXCLUSIVE DESIGN
By Mark Stewart

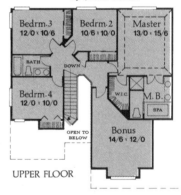

UPPER FLOOR

QUIET LIVING LAYOUT

DESIGN NO. 91642

- This plan features:
- — Two bedrooms
- — Two full baths
- A covered Entry leading to the back of the home
- Living/Dining area with built-in shelves, loads of windows and access to the back yard
- An open Kitchen with an island cooktop adjacent to the laundry, Garage and Dining/Living area
- A Master suite with a decorative window topped by a coved ceiling, an oversized closet and a private bath with a dressing table and a roll-in shower
- Accessibility Features:
- — Level entry way
- — Wide doorways (32"-36" clear width)
- — Chair height electrical controls/outlets
- — Reinforced walls for installation of grab bars

No. 91642

MAIN FLOOR

MAIN FLOOR — 1,295 SQ. FT

TOTAL LIVING AREA:
1,295 SQ. FT.

An
EXCLUSIVE DESIGN
By Mark Stewart

No materials list available

PRICE CODE B

UNUSUAL CEILINGS ADD ELEGANCE

DESIGN NO. 91644

- This plan features:
- — Two bedrooms
- — Two full baths
- A covered entrance into the Foyer with sliding glass doors to a private terrace and connecting the Living and Dining Rooms
- A vaulted ceiling in the Living Room accenting a recessed, decorative window and a large hearth fireplace set between two more decorative windows
- An efficient Kitchen with a cooktop/eating island opening to the Family Room with a coved ceiling and sliding glass doors to a covered porch
- A Master suite with a decorative window topped by a coved ceiling, a walk-in closet and a private bath with a double vanity
- French doors leading into a Den/Bedroom with a double closet
- Accessibility Features:
- — Level entry way
- — Wide doorways (32"-36" clear width)
- — Chair height electrical controls/outlets
- — Reinforced walls for installation of grab bars

MAIN FLOOR — 1,687 SQ. FT.

TOTAL LIVING AREA:
1,687 SQ. FT.

An
EXCLUSIVE DESIGN
By Mark Stewart

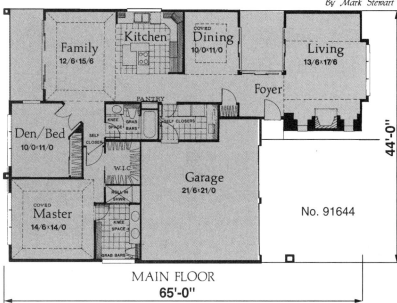

MAIN FLOOR
65'-0"

No materials list available

PRICE CODE A

PRICE CODE D

No. 91684

■ This plan features:

— Three bedrooms

— Two and a half baths

■ A coved ceiling in the Living Room and expansive windows in both the formal Dining and Living Rooms

■ A tiled Family Room with a corner fireplace and a sliding glass door to the Deck

■ An Kitchen with a corner window, a large pantry and a peninsula cooktop counter to serve the Nook and Family Room

■ A Master Suite with a wall of windows

■ Accessibility Features:

— Level entry way

— Wide doorways (32"-36" clear width)

— Chair height electrical controls/outlets

— Reinforced walls for installation of grab bars

FIRST FLOOR — 1,632 SQ. FT.
SECOND FLOOR — 776 SQ. FT.

TOTAL LIVING AREA:
2,408 SQ. FT.

ACCESSIBILITY IN MIND

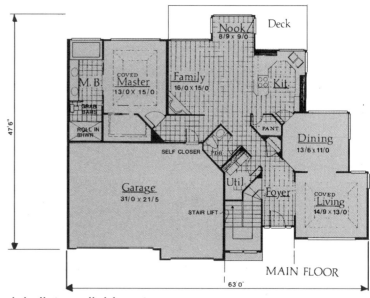

MAIN FLOOR

No materials list available

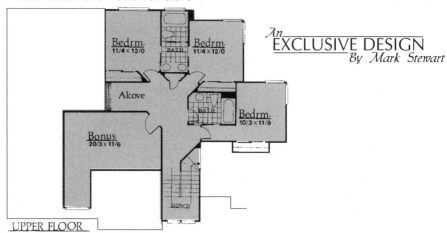

An
EXCLUSIVE DESIGN
By Mark Stewart

UPPER FLOOR

Ignoring Copyright Laws Can Be A $1,000,000 Mistake

Recent changes in the US copyright laws allow for statutory penalties of up to **$100,000** per incident for copyright infringement involving any of the copyrighted plans found in this publication. The law can be confusing. So, for your own protection, take the time to understand what you can and cannot do when it comes to home plans.

—— *What You Cannot Do* ——

You Cannot Duplicate Home Plans

Purchasing a set of blueprints and making additional sets by reproducing the original is *illegal*. If you need multiple sets of a particular home plan, then you must purchase them.

You Cannot Copy Any Part of a Home Plan to Create Another

Creating your own plan by copying even part of a home design found in this publication is called "creating a derivative work" and is *illegal* unless you have permission to do so.

You Cannot Build a Home Without a License

You must have specific permission or license to build a home from a copyrighted design, even if the finished home has been changed from the original plan. It is *illegal* to build one of the homes found in this publication without a license.

What Garlinghouse Offers

Home Plan Blueprint Package

By purchasing a single or multiple set package of blueprints from Garlinghouse, you not only receive the physical blueprint documents necessary for construction, but you are also granted a license to build one, and only one, home. You can also make any changes to our design that you wish, as long as these changes are made directly on the blueprints purchased from Garlinghouse and no additional copies are made.

Home Plan Vellums

By purchasing vellums for one of our home plans, you receive the same construction drawings found in the blueprints, but printed on vellum paper. Vellums can be erased and are perfect for making design changes. They are also semi-transparent making them easy to duplicate. But most importantly, the purchase of home plan vellums comes with a broader license that allows you to make changes to the design (ie, create a hand drawn or CAD derivative work), to make an unlimited number of copies of the plan, and to build up to three homes from the plan.

License To Build Additional Homes

With the purchase of a blueprint package or vellums you automatically receive a license to build one home or three homes, respectively. If you want to build more homes than you are licensed to build through your purchase of a plan, then additional licenses may be purchased at reasonable costs from Garlinghouse. Inquire for more information.

Everything You Need to M
You pay only a fraction of the original cost

You've Picked Your Dream Home!

You can already see it standing on your lot... you can see yourselves in your new home... enjoying family, entertaining guests, celebrating holidays. All that remains ahead are the details. That's where we can help. Whether you plan to build-it-yourself, be your own contractor, or hand your plans over to an outside contractor, your Garlinghouse blueprints provide the perfect beginning for putting yourself in your dream home right away.

We even make it simple for you to make professional design modifications. We can also provide a materials list for greater economy.

My grandfather, L.F. Garlinghouse, started a tradition of quality when he founded this company in 1907. For over 85 years, homeowners and builders have relied on us for accurate, complete, professional blueprints. Our plans help you get results fast... and save money, too! These pages will give you all the information you need to order. So get started now... I know you'll love your new Garlinghouse home!

Sincerely,

TYPICAL WALL SECTIONS

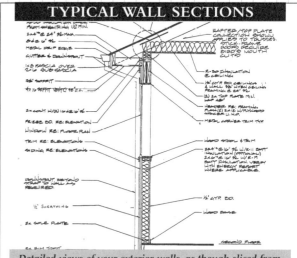

Detailed views of your exterior walls, as though sliced from top to bottom. These drawings clarify exterior wall construction insulation, flooring, and roofing details. Depending on your specific geography and climate, your home will be built with either 2x4 or 2x6 exterior walls. Most professional contractors can easily adapt plans for either requirement.

KITCHEN & BATH CABINET DETAILS

These plans or, in some cases, elevations show the specific details and placement of the cabinets in your kitchen and bathrooms as applicable. Customizing these areas is simpler beginning with these details. Kitchen and bath cabinet details are available for most plans featured in our collection.

EXTERIOR ELEVATIONS

Exact scale views of the front, rear and both sides of your home, showing exterior materials, details, and all necessary measurements.

DETAILED FLOOR PLANS

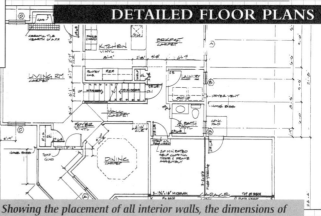

Showing the placement of all interior walls, the dimensions of rooms, doors, windows, stairways, and other details.

ake Your Dream Come True!

for home designs by respected professionals.

FIREPLACE DETAILS

When your home includes one or more fireplaces, these detailed drawings will help your mason with their construction and appearance. It is easy to review details with professionals when you have the plans for reference.

TYPICAL CROSS SECTION

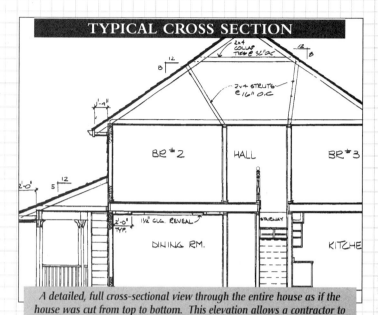

A detailed, full cross-sectional view through the entire house as if the house was cut from top to bottom. This elevation allows a contractor to better understand the interconnections of the construction components.

FOUNDATION PLAN

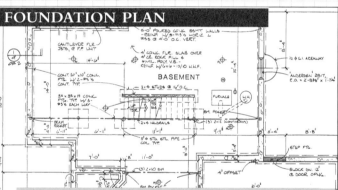

With footings and all load-bearing points applicable to your home, including all necessary notation and dimensions. The type of foundation supplied varies from home to home. Local conditions and practices will determine whether a basement, crawlspace or a slab is best for you. Your professional contractor can easily make the necessary adaption.

SCHEMATIC ELECTRICAL LAYOUTS

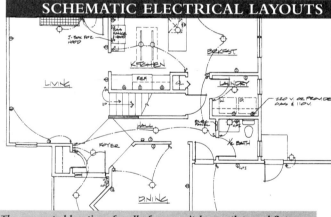

The suggested locations for all of your switches, outlets and fixtures are indicated on these drawings. They are practical as they are, but they are also a solid taking-off point for any personal adaptions.

ROOF PLAN

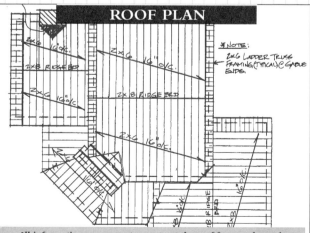

All information necessary to construct the roof for your home is included. Many blueprints contain framing plans showing all of the roof elements, so you'll know how these details look and fit together.

STAIR DETAILS

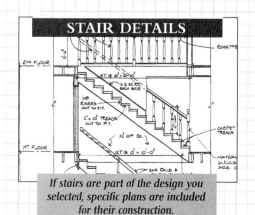

If stairs are part of the design you selected, specific plans are included for their construction.

GARLINGHOUSE OPTIONS & EXTRAS
MAKE THE DREAM TRULY YOURS.

Reversed Plans Can Make Your Dream Home Just Right!

"That's our dream home... if only the garage were on the other side!"

You could have exactly the home you want by flipping it end-for-end. Check it out by holding your dream home page of this book up to a mirror. Then simply order your plans "reversed". We'll send you one full set of mirror-image plans (with the writing backwards) as a master guide for you and your builder.

The remaining sets of your order will come as shown in this book so the dimensions and specifications are easily read on the job site... but they will be specially stamped "REVERSED" so there is no construction confusion.

We can only send reversed plans with multiple-set orders. But, there is no extra charge for this service.

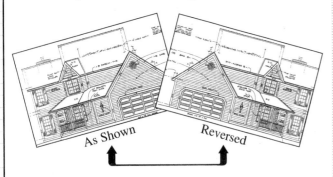

As Shown   Reversed

Modifying Your Garlinghouse Home Plan

Easy modifications to your dream home such as minor non-structural changes and simple material substitutions, can be made between you and your builder and marked directly on your blueprints. However, if you are considering making major changes to your design, we strongly recommend that you purchase our reproducible vellums and use the services of a professional designer or architect. For additional information call us at 1-860-343-5977.

Our Reproducible Vellums Make Modifications Easier

With a vellum copy of our plans, a design professional can alter the drawings just the way you want, then you can print as many copies of the modified plans as you need. And, since you have already started with our complete detailed plans, the cost of those expensive professional services will be significantly less. Refer to the price schedule for vellum costs. Call for vellum availability for plan numbers 90,000 and above.

Reproducible vellum copies of our home plans are only sold under the terms of a license agreement that you will receive with your order. Should you not agree to the terms, then the vellums may be returned unopened for a full refund.

Yours FREE With Your Order

FREE
SPECIFICATIONS AND CONTRACT FORM

provides the perfect way for you and your builder to agree on the exact materials to use in building and finishing your home before you start construction. A must for homeowner's peace of mind.

Remember To Order Your Materials List

It'll help you save money. Available at a modest additional charge, the Materials List gives the quantity, dimensions, and specifications for the major materials needed to build your home. You will get faster, more accurate bids from your contractors and building suppliers — and avoid paying for unused materials and waste. Materials Lists are available for all home plans except as otherwise indicated, but can only be ordered with a set of home plans. Due to differences in regional requirements and homeowner or builder preferences... electrical, plumbing and heating/air conditioning equipment specifications are not designed specifically for each plan. However, non plan specific detailed typical prints of residential electrical, plumbing and construction guidelines can be provided. Please see next page for additional information.

Questions?

Call our customer service number at 1-860-343-5977.

How Many Sets Of Plans Will You Need?

The Standard 8-Set Construction Package

Our experience shows that you'll speed every step of construction and avoid costly building errors by ordering enough sets to go around. Each tradesperson wants a set — the general contractor and all subcontractors; foundation, electrical, plumbing, heating/air conditioning, drywall, finish carpenters, and cabinet shop. Don't forget your lending institution, building department and, of course, a set for yourself.

The Minimum 5-Set Construction Package

If you're comfortable with arduous follow-up, this package can save you a few dollars by giving you the option of passing down plan sets as work progresses. You might have enough copies to go around if work goes exactly as scheduled and no plans are lost or damaged. But for only $50 more, the 8-set package eliminates these worries.

The Single-Set Decision-Maker Package

We offer this set so you can study the blueprints to plan your dream home in detail. But remember... one set is never enough to build your home... and they're copyrighted.

New Plan Details For The Home Builder

Because local codes and requirements vary greatly, we recommend that you obtain drawings and bids from licensed contractors to do your mechanical plans. However, if you want to know more about techniques — and deal more confidently with subcontractors — we offer these remarkably useful detail sheets. Each is an excellent tool that will enhance your understanding of these technical subjects.

Residential Construction Details

Eight sheets that cover the essentials of stick-built residential home construction. Details foundation options - poured concrete basement, concrete block, or monolithic concrete slab. Shows all aspects of floor, wall, and roof framing. Provides details for roof dormers, eaves, and skylights. Conforms to requirements of Uniform Building code or BOCA code. Includes a quick index.

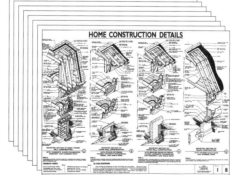

$14.95 per set

Residential Plumbing Details

Nine sheets packed with information detailing pipe connection methods, fittings, and sizes. Shows sump-pump and water softener hookups, and septic system construction. Conforms to requirements of National Plumbing Code. Color coded with a glossary of terms and quick index.

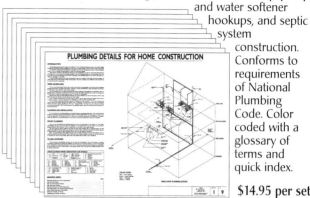

$14.95 per set

Residential Electrical Details

Nine sheets that cover all aspects of residential wiring, from simple switch wiring to the complexities of three-phase and service entrance connection. Explains service load calculations and distribution panel wiring. Shows you how to create a floor-plan wiring diagram. Conforms to requirements of National Electrical Code. Color coded with a glossary of terms and a quick index.

$14.95 per set

Important Shipping Information

Your order is processed immediately. Allow 10 working days from our receipt of your order for normal ground delivery. Save time with your credit card and our "800" number. Our delivery service must have a street address or Rural Route Box number — never a post office box. Use a work address if no one is home during the day.

Orders being shipped to Alaska, Hawaii, APO, FPO or Post Office Boxes must go via First Class Mail. Please include the proper postage.

Only Certified bank checks and money orders are accepted and must be payable in U.S. currency. For speed, we ship international orders Air Parcel Post. Please refer to the chart for the correct shipping cost.

An important note:

All plans are drawn to conform to one or more of the industry's major national building standards. However, due to the variety of local building regulations, your plan may need to be modified to comply with local requirements — snow loads, energy loads, seismic zones, etc. Do check them fully and consult your local building officials.

A few states require that all building plans used be drawn by an architect registered in that state. While having your plans reviewed and stamped by such an architect may be prudent, laws requiring non-conforming plans like ours to be completely redrawn forces you to unnecessarily pay very large fees. If your state has such a law, we strongly recommend you contact your state representative to protest.

BEFORE ORDERING PLEASE READ ALL ORDERING INFORMATION

Please submit all Canadian plan orders to:
Garlinghouse Company
20 Cedar Street North, Kitchener, Ontario N2H 2W8
Canadian Customers Only: 1-800-561-4169/Fax #: 1-519-743-1282
Customer Service #: 1-519-743-4169

ORDER TOLL FREE— 1-800-235-5700
Monday-Friday 8:00 a.m. to 5:00 p.m. Eastern Time
or FAX your Credit Card order to 1-203-343-5984
All foreign residents call 1-203-343-5977

Please have ready: 1. *Your credit card number* 2. *The plan number* 3. *The order code number* ⇨ **H5VL4**

GARLINGHOUSE BLUEPRINT PRICE CODE SCHEDULE:
Additional sets with original order $25

PRICE CODE	A	B	C	D	E	F	G	H
8 SETS OF SAME PLAN	$330	$350	$375	$400	$430	$470	$510	$555
5 SETS OF SAME PLAN	$280	$300	$325	$350	$380	$420	$460	$505
1 SINGLE SET OF PLANS	$210	$230	$255	$280	$310	$350	$390	$435
VELLUMS	$420	$440	$465	$490	$520	$560	$600	$645
MATERIALS LIST	$25	$25	$30	$30	$35	$40	$40	$45

DOMESTIC SHIPPING*	1-2 Sets	3+ Sets
UPS/RPS Ground Service	$6.50	$8.50
First Class Mail	$8.00	$11.00
2-Day Express	$16.00	$20.00
Overnight Express	$26.00	$30.00

INTERNATIONAL SHIPPING	1-2 Sets	3+ Sets
Canada	**$11.00**	**$15.50**
All Other Nations	$40.00	$52.00

*Plan Numbers 90,000 & Above For Domestic Shipping — Standard Express 3-5 Days -- $20.00

Canadian Orders and Shipping: To our friends in Canada, we have a plan design affiliate in Kitchener, Ontario. This relationship will help you avoid the delays and charges associated with shipments from the United States. Moreover, our affiliate is familiar with the building requirements in your community and country. We prefer payments in U.S. Currency. If you, however, are sending Canadian funds please add 40% to the prices of the plans and shipping fees.

─ Blueprint Order Form ─ Order Code No. **H5VL4**

Plan No. _____
❏ As Shown   ❏ Reversed *(mult. set pkgs. only)*

	Each	Amount
8 set pkg.		$
5 set pkg.		$
1 set pkg. (no reverses)		$
_____ (qty.) Add'l. sets @		$
Vellums		$
Materials List (with plan order only)		$
Residential Builder Plans		
_____ set(s) Construction	@ $14.95	$
_____ set(s) Plumbing	@ $14.95	$
_____ set(s) Electrical	@ $14.95	$
Shipping		$
Subtotal		$
Sales Tax (CT residents add 6% sales tax, KS residents add 6.15% sales tax) (Not required for other states)		$
Total Amount Enclosed		**$**

Prices guaranteed until 11-15-96
Payment must be made in U.S. funds
Foreign Mail Orders: Certified bank checks in U.S. funds only

Credit Card Information
Charge To: ❏ Visa   ❏ Mastercard

Card # |_|_|_|_|_|_|_|_|_|_|_|_|_|_|_|_|

Signature _____ Exp. _____ / _____

Send your check, money order or credit card information to:
(No C.O.D.'s Please)
Please Submit all <u>United States</u> & <u>Other Nations</u> plan orders to:
Garlinghouse Company
P.O. Box 1717
Middletown, CT 06457

Please Submit all <u>Canadian</u> plan orders to:
Garlinghouse Company
20 Cedar Street North
Kitchener, Ontario N2H 2W8

Bill To: (address must be as it appears on credit card statement)

Name_____

Address_____

City/State_____ Zip_____

Daytime Phone (_____) _____

Ship To (if different from Bill to):

Name_____

Address_____

City/State_____ Zip_____

TERMS OF SALE FOR HOME PLANS:
All home plans sold through this publication are copyright protected. Reproduction of these home plans, either in whole or in part, including any direct copying and/or preparation of derivative works thereof, for any reason without the prior written permission of The L.F. Garlinghouse Co., Inc., is strictly prohibited. The purchase of a set of home plans in no way transfers any copyright or other ownership interest in it to the buyer except for a limited license to use that set of home plans for the construction of one, and only one, dwelling unit. The purchase of additional sets of that home plan at a reduced price from the original set or as a part of a multiple set package does not entitle the buyer with a license to construct more than one dwelling unit.